LAW AND ECONOMICS

A Comparative Approach to Theory and Practice

By
Robin Paul Malloy
Professor of Law and Economics
College of Law, Syracuse University

WEST PUBLISHING CO.
ST. PAUL, MINN.
1990

COPYRIGHT © 1990 By WEST PUBLISHING CO.
50 West Kellogg Boulevard
P.O. Box 64526
St. Paul, MN 55164–0526

Library of Congress Cataloging-in-Publication Data

ISBN 0–314–72586–5

Malloy–Law & Econ.Misc.

For Margaret Ann

*

Preface

This book emerged as an idea over the course of several years of writing and teaching in the area of law and economics. I would teach seminars in law and economics and write in the area but still be unable to point people to a comprehensive yet simple introductory text on the subject of law and economics. In the few pages that make up this book my goal is to provide an introductory guide to students, lawyers, professors, and all others that seek a general understanding of the relationship between law and economics.

Since I have a broad view of what the study of law and economics involves I tried to make this book as inclusive as possible. The book, while serving as an introduction to the relationship between law and economics, is more than a mere descriptive undertaking. The overall approach to the subject matter and the ideological distinctions drawn in this book are central to my own work in creating a new way of thinking about law and economics. From this perspective I try to provide an introduction to a variety of views concerning the relationship between law and economics, and in this light the book presents a brief discussion of the views of conservatives, liberals, left communitarians and neo-marxists, libertarians, and classical liberals. In these few pages it is likely that a follower of any one of these philosophical traditions will think I have left much unsaid. However, I have tried to fairly present the core distinctions and values that separate these groups so that the reader can see the general themes at work in each competing theory of the relationship between law and economics.

In addition to providing a general introduction to basic economics and to the primary ideological traditions in which debates on law and economics occur, I have tried to provide a list of suggested readings at the end of each chapter which will allow readers to pursue more detailed studies in accordance with their own interests and time constraints. With a selection of articles from the various suggested readings, this text can serve as the core organizer of a seminar in law and economics. At the same time, the book can be used as a helpful supplement to other courses in terms of introducing the basics of law and economics in a context of other competing theories of thought.

Finally, the book contains a section that involves a study of leading cases. The cases chosen for inclusion in this book represent several topic areas of law (contracts, property, torts, etc.). I tried to select cases that would make good illustrations of competing theories at work in a practical setting of application and which would likely be familiar to many students of the law. The idea of the cases is to show how the general theories discussed in the book can be applied in the practice of law. The struggle between competing philosophies of law, in other words, is not merely a matter of theory.

My hope is that this book will serve as a brief but useful introduction to a complex new age of legal theory. That this book will provide the kind of broad based introduction and follow up suggested readings that will make it an affordable and efficient resource for people that simply want to know what law and economics is all about. It is in this spirit that I conceived this book and it is with the help of West Publishing Company that this idea has become a reality.

In preparing this book I received invaluable help and comments from a number of people. I wish to thank Professors Paul Cox, Jonathan Turley, and Alan Childress for their review and comments on an early draft. Also, a special thanks to my general research assistant Joe McGlinchey, and to Linda Eppen, a former research assistant that assisted in the preparation of material for the chapter on basic economics and who assembled The Glossary of Economic Terms. Finally, I thank the word processing staff at

Tulane Law School for their cooperative efforts while I was
on the Tulane Faculty.

ROBIN PAUL MALLOY
Syracuse, New York

*

Summary of Contents

Table of Contents

*

Table of Cases

The principal cases are in bold type. Cases cited or discussed in the text are in roman type. References are to pages. Cases cited in principal cases and within other quoted materials are not included.

*

LAW AND ECONOMICS

A Comparative Approach to Theory and Practice

Part One
BACKGROUND AND PERSPECTIVE

Chapter One

LAW AND ECONOMICS— A COMPARATIVE APPROACH

Legal literature is replete with references to law and economics and to an economic analysis of law. In the years since Richard Posner completed his first edition of ECONOMIC ANALYSIS OF LAW, numerous articles have been written about the application of economic methods to the resolution of complex social and legal problems.[1] In addition, many law professors have developed courses identified as Law and Economics or Economic Analysis of Law. But what are these courses and what are they teaching us about the relationship between law and economics? To begin to understand the answer to this question one must first understand the distinction between the terms "law and economics" and "an economic analysis of law."

The study of law and economics should be comparative in nature. It should focus on the relationship between economic philosophy, political philosophy, and legal philosophy as they relate to alternative social arrangements. In a nutshell, one must learn to appreciate the fact that a person with a marxist view of political and economic arrangements will have a different view of law and legal process than will a person oriented towards free market and capitalist thinking. The recog-

---

1. R. Posner, ECONOMIC ANALYSIS OF LAW (1986) (1st ed. 1972).

nition of this simple point is important in as much as the reading of judicial opinions, the characterization of legal claims before certain types of judges, and the formality of legal argument in general is in great part influenced by ideological visions of the economic and political relationships that promote the "just" society.

In contrast to this overriding ideological and comparative approach to law and economics, the economic analysis of law is primarily concerned with using economic methods as theoretical constructs for analyzing, in economic terms, the rules and laws adopted by a particular society. In this sense, what generally passes under the rubric of economic analysis of law is, for our purposes, only one component of a much richer study of comparative perspectives that should include an introduction to such contemporary subdisciplines as critical legal studies, conservative, liberal, libertarian, and classical liberal theory, among others. Economic analysis of law, by subjecting legal doctrine to economic cost and benefit analysis and to concepts of economic efficiency, can allow us to draw certain conclusions about the consequences and alleged social value of particular legal arrangements. It can be argued, for instance, that certain rules of tort liability or of contract damages improperly assign legal consequences to the party least able or least likely to respond in the desired social manner. Likewise, economic methods can be used to evaluate the likely behavioral response to changes in the severity of criminal sanctions or to changes in the tax laws or to changes in real or personal property law.

In each instance of economic analysis the values of the neoclassical economic model are assumed as given and the current or proposed law is analyzed within the given social framework. Such an economic approach allows for an evaluation of the descriptive consequences of a legal rule while also making it possible to assert a limited range of normative arguments about the desirability of a continuation of or a change in that rule. Such an economic analysis of law, however, is too narrow a method of inquiry for today's lawyers. In today's legal environment a lawyer must not only be able to recharacterize her client's case from one sounding in contract for breach of warranty to one sounding in tort for negligence, but she must also be able to recharacterize the underlying philosophical justifications for her legal arguments depending upon whether her audience is more or less sympathic to anyone of a competing number of legal schools of thought. These competing views on legal thought are inevitably linked to underlying beliefs concerning such things as conservative, liberal, left communitarian, libertarian or classical liberal values.

The proper study of law and economics should, therefore, require us to evaluate alternative social arrangements while exploring the consequences that such alternatives have on the relationship between law and economics. Whereas an economic analysis of law involves the use of economic methods to analyze legal rules and relationships within a particular society, law and economics should be concerned with contrasting and comparing alternative social arrangements across a political and economic spectrum that encompasses multiple models of the "just" society. Law and economics does not, therefore, concentrate on analyzing, by economic methods, the efficiency of numerous legal rules generated by a given society. Rather, the primary goal of law and economics should be to investigate how certain values or principles will be affected by changing a community's current social, political, and economic arrangements. This method of inquiry leads to a more philosophical and humanistic approach than does the more limited study of an economic analysis of law.

Consequently, this method of inquiry is also more consistent with the way in which lawyers, law professors and law students approach other areas of legal study such as jurisprudence.

As a comparative study, law and economics provides an opportunity to view legal arrangements as a reflection of a particular political ideology. Diverse ideological values can be contrasted and compared by unmasking their presence in current legal arrangements. A critical evaluation of these legal arrangements and of their underlying political ideology is important because it not only reveals where we have been but also where we are going with the evolution of our law and our society.

Selecting the core values that will be the subject of one's critical comparative evaluation, should not be difficult. One could, for example, focus on classical liberal philosophy and on its core values of morality, individual liberty and human dignity. On the other hand, one could as easily select a core value not of individual liberty but of altruistic communitarianism and achieve the same comparative benefits. This is possible because the study of law and economics, as described here, does not test legal rules solely for their tendency towards economic efficiency, but rather considers the political, economic and historical context of legal arrangements in order to see how their current configuration affects the underlying value chosen for consideration.

Within the context of a course in law and economics, one must provide critical analysis of how certain values would be affected by alternative legal arrangements which embrace different sets of political and economic norms. Thus, one must ask, for example, how the classical liberal concern for individual liberty would be affected by alternative legal arrangements reflecting, democratic-capitalist norms, democratic socialist norms, marxist-communitarian norms, state-capitalist norms, or neo-fascist norms, among others. Likewise, one achieves the same academic benefit from this comparative method of analysis even if the core value is altruistic communitarianism rather than individual liberty. While the academic benefits may be the same, however, the conclusions drawn from the critical evaluation may be different. This is possible because a change in the core value to be promoted can result in different conclusions about the viability or acceptability of particular social, political, economic, and legal arrangements.

In the process of doing the comparative critique described above, one must analyze the actual legal arrangements being made in a society nurtured on a given political ideology, such as free market capitalism, in order to see if the "in fact" legal structure is consistent with the community's political rhetoric. One may find that the legal structure is in fact inconsistent with the political rhetoric embraced by the society. In such a case the reasons for the inconsistency can be evaluated in both political and economic terms. In addition, exposure of the inconsistency should lead to a critical evaluation of the proper manner in which an informed choice might lead the community to a restructuring of their own communal order. They may decide to relinquish "outdated" norms so as to recognize the newly emerging norms inherent in their current legal arrangements or instead; they may decide to reject the encroachment by new norms upon existing norms that are still highly valued. The important point should be that the community, and especially the lawyers within that community, need to know and appreciate the way in which alternative legal arrangements affect underlying values, such as individual liberty, and alternatively, how different values, such as altruistic communitarianism rather than individual liberty, affect the spectrum of appropriate legal arrangements.

An example of this approach may be useful. Consider the city of Indianapolis, Indiana.[2] Indianapolis is a city of about one million people located in the "heart" of the "heartland." It is a community where most of the people take pride in traditional, conservative, republican values. They value hard work, capitalism, the free market, and rugged individualism. In dramatic contrast to the spoken rhetoric of these "down home" values, however, Hoosiers in the state's capital city live under a rather different set of political, legal, and economic norms. In a quest for urban revitalization the city has worked hard to come up with creative financing and legal arrangements that have helped change the city skyline, and, some would say, improve the quality of life. But, the underlying philosophical change in community norms has gone essentially unnoticed and consequently unevaluated.

While most Indianapolis lawyers, politicians, and business people have focused their attention on "how to get the job done," no one has reflected on the issue of how certain methods of getting the job done may affect underlying community norms. Thus, in a city where private property, free enterprise, and the individual entrepreneur stand as rhetorically supreme, the reality is that most of the commercial real estate activity in the downtown area is heavily subsidized, administered by central planning boards, and owned in some significant way by the "state." The realities of this "state capital-

---

2. *See*, Malloy, *The Political Economy of Co-financing America's Urban Renaissance*, 40 VAND.L.REV. 67 (1987). *See also*, R.P. Malloy, PLANNING FOR SERFDOM—A CONTEXTUAL THEORY OF LAW, ECONOMICS AND THE STATE (Forthcoming, from the Univ. of Penn. Press, 1990).

ism" or "urban socialism," seem to stand in dramatic contrast to the rhetoric and self image of most residents of the Hoosier state. The merits of such redevelopment programs should be the focus of intense debate about underlying values, but before people can decide either to discard old norms or to reject new norms they must realize the extent to which their social, political, economic, and legal arrangements are reflective of a particular underlying ideology.

The comparative study of law and economics should prepare one to engage in this critical evaluation process. In studying the relationship between law and economics one must learn to be critical, in the sense that one must come to understand the way in which their own political and economic ideology reflects and is reflected in their understanding and use of law. Furthermore, the student of law and economics must come to grips with alternative ideologies so that they can engage in a meaningful dialogue about the proper values to be furthered by membership in a community and the proper means for attaining those values. Considered in this light, there is a very real difference between the study of law and economics and the methods of an economic analysis of law.

The study of law and economics is not a study in law and politics although there are obvious interrelationships. In the comparative study of law and economics, economic philosophy should be the focal point for critical evaluation of law, politics, and society. Analysis should center on the relationship between law and economics within particular political settings. Rather than focusing on the political theory behind alternative social arrangements, this approach puts emphasis on the evaluation of how legal arrangements are inherently connected to economic philosophy.

A marxist vision of the proper economic arrangements between members of a given society, for instance, would be different than the corresponding vision held by, say, a conservative "Reagan Republican" or a "Chicago School" economist. Consequently, the legal, political, and social arrangements that correspond to the underlying economic philosophy would be different. Because of this, one can observe that culturally based legal arrangements are shaped by the economic philosophy of the community and are reflected in that society's conception of law and justice. In this context, then, the student of law and economics should begin to appreciate the dynamic interaction between law, politics, and economics as it is manifested through alternative ideologies.

Likewise, the comparative study of law and economics is not merely a study of jurisprudence. The study of law and economics involves the investigation of the relationship between economic and legal conceptions of the "good" and "just" society. It does not, at a primary level, involve the search for "what is law" nor does it involve a study of the history of legal theory. Naturally, such concerns are related to a study of law and economics but they are not the focal point of such study. This position can be easily understood by an analogy to the course in real property law. While it can be said that constitutional law underlies many of our conceptions of real property it is also true that the course in real property is not merely a repetition of the course in constitutional law. In the same way, the comparative study of law and economics is fundamentally different from the study of jurisprudence.

Having described the general nature of a comparative approach to the study of law and economics, I will briefly describe the layout and plan for the remainder of the book. Conceived primarily as an introductory source for the study of emerging and competing schools of legal economic thought, the book seeks first to present a generalized version of these alternative approaches and secondly to show how these alternative approaches can be put to practical use in improving one's lawyering skills.

Since this book deals with the relationship between law and economics and assumes its readers are more familiar with law than with economics, it begins with a basic introduction to economics for the non-economist. This introduction presents a general overview of basic economic methods and terminology. The introduction should be viewed as the doorway to resolving definitional problems before entering into the hallway of comparative analysis. From this starting point, the following chapter will consider the inherent value judgments that are present in models of economic analysis. This chapter is designed to disabuse the reader, at the outset, of the notion that economics is a neutral and objective science. To the contrary, economics, like law, is fundamentally a philosophically and ideologically based undertaking. Thus, "marxist" economics is different than "Keynesian" economics, and both are different from "Chicago School" economics.

After establishing a foundation, by way of the introductory material in chapters two and three, the book will discuss a number of subtopic areas that will serve as introductions to comparative views of law and economics. The introduction to comparative approaches of law and economics is in chapters four through eight and is arranged along five separate subtopics of inquiry. Each of the five chapters involves a different philosophical and ideological approach to the relationship between legal and economic conceptions of the good and just society. Chapter four involves a study of the "conservative" philosophical approach to law and to economics. It is within this philosophical context that the book will discuss the economic analysis of law as practiced by its chief spokesperson, Judge Richard Posner. The fifth chapter of study focuses on "liberal" perspectives of law and economics. This part of the book looks at the political and ideological approaches that support what is sometimes referred to as the "welfare state." The sixth chapter involves an introduction to the Critical Legal Studies (CLS) movement. While the CLS authors are by no means writing in a unified voice they do tend to present a perspective that is philosophically neo-marxist and "left-communitarian," and which is overwhelmingly antagonistic to the economic analysis of law. The seventh chapter of study concerns "libertarian" philosophy and its relevancy to an understanding of the relationship between law and economics. This subtopic of study can provide an interesting critique of both liberal and conservative perspectives while focusing on the "proper" role of law in the promotion of individual rights within a framework of limited government. The eighth chapter of study considers law and economics in light of "classical liberal" theory. Classical liberal theory is in some respects similar to libertarianism but at the same time it is different in that it can perceive of, and justify, a much greater role for governmental involvement in the economic life of society.

After a general introduction to each of these comparative approaches, chapters nine through thirteen of the book will show how these theoretical perspectives can actually work into a practical understanding of law. In this context a review of five leading cases will be presented. Following this discussion chapter fourteen of the book will present some concluding comments on the practical nature of and need for enhancing one's understanding of the general theoretical debates in this area.

Throughout the book references will be made to sources for additional reading. Given the brevity and the introductory nature of this book, it is impossible to present all of the detailed distinctions that exists between the numerous scholars writing in any given philosophical mode. Likewise, no particular effort is made to segregate emerging feminist theory into a separate chapter of discussion. This has been done on the belief that feminist theory can best be understood as a feminist perspective within any possible or potential school of economic philosophy and ideology. Feminist theory, in other words, is not necessarily libertarian or neomarxist for instance, but on the contrary can be ideologically diverse. References to feminist works are included at various points throughout the book.

Within the constraints set out here, the book will outline the general contours of the basic competing theories in this area and will hopefully serve as a convenient and useful introduction to the understanding of both traditional economic analysis of law and the more comparative conception of law and economics.

Suggested Reading

Books

J. Galbraith, ECONOMICS IN PERSPECTIVE: A CRITICAL HISTORY (1987).

C. Goetz, LAW AND ECONOMICS (1984).

T. Machan, THE MAIN DEBATE: COMMUNISM VERSUS CAPITALISM (1987).

H. Manne, THE ECONOMICS OF LEGAL RELATIONSHIPS (1975).

J. Schumpeter, CAPITALISM, SOCIALISM AND DEMOCRACY (1947).

ECONOMIC IMPERIALISM: THE ECONOMIC METHOD APPLIED OUTSIDE THE FIELD OF ECONOMICS (G. Radnitzky & P. Bernholz eds. 1987).

FREEDOM AND VIRTUE—THE CONSERVATIVE/LIBERTARIAN DEBATE (G. Carey ed. 1984).

Chapter Two
BASIC ECONOMICS FOR LAW AND ECONOMICS

Before we can assess the value of economics to the study of law we must first have a basic understanding of what economics is.

Alfred Marshall, the British economist responsible for economics' emphasis for the past 100 years on the principles of supply and demand, has said: "Economics is a study of mankind in the ordinary business of life." The study of economics involves the making of certain assumptions which allow us to make predictions about outcomes when certain variables are manipulated. From a narrow perspective, these variables may be changes in the money supply, interest rates, or other financial factors. But for the economist—the study of economics goes beyond finance and business and as such, changes in variables such as laws, customs, and other aspects of daily life can be studied and analyzed for predictable effects. It will be our task to see how law can be studied within this framework, thereby allowing us to make policy arguments and legal arguments for or against any given legislation or court decision.

There are two basic premises of economics: scarcity and rationality.

SCARCITY

A fundamental principle of economics is that there is scarcity. Scarcity reflects the unlimited nature of human wants. That is to say, we can think of more goods and services we would like than we can actually afford. On a personal level scarcity simply means that with an income of $20,000 you may want to buy a three bedroom home, buy a Porsche sports car, take a trip to Europe, go to a movie once a week, eat out three times a week, and send $1,000 home to your sick mother. You just can't do everything with your $20,000.

The Federal Government has the same problem. It takes in $200 billion in tax revenue but wants to spend much more than that on the military, welfare programs, space exploration, dam building, etc.

The existence of scarcity means that choices must be made, i.e. if you can't have everything on your dream list but can have some of it, what do you choose?

RATIONALITY

Rationality means that in the choice process confronting us because of scarcity, people will act in a manner that they believe gives them the best combination of desirable results within the confines of their resources. The rational economic person is possibly analogous to the reasonably prudent person in law in the following sense: For economic theory to have relevance and to be a good predictor we do not need to show that every person is always rational in the economic sense. As long as most people will act rationally much of the time, it doesn't affect our general predictive abilities to know that some people are self destructive, under the influence of drugs or mind control, or anything else.

Significantly, the rationality of any given course of action does not depend on the actual choice made but rather on the process by which the choice was made. Therefore, it is entirely possible for two individuals to make different choices, and yet for each individual to be acting rationally.

Example: 'A' and 'B' both have $20,000, and each would like to buy a new car and a new boat this year. In their world of car and boat sales, a full-size car costs $20,000, a smaller car costs $10,000, and a boat costs $10,000. 'A' buys the full-size car for $20,000 and 'B' buys the smaller car and the boat for $20,000. Have both 'A' and 'B' acted rationally?

Yes. 'A' values the full-size car more than the smaller car and the boat combined. Many people own extremely expensive cars even though if they bought a cheaper car they could afford to buy other goods and services. Maybe a full-size car is important to 'A' for prestige or to impress clients, or 'A' does a lot of long distance driving, or 'A' was previously a victim of a serious car accident in which the other driver in a small car was killed and 'A' is convinced that he was saved by virtue of being in a full-size car. 'B' on the other hand has a different set of values. Both 'A' and 'B' act rationally because they each set out to obtain what they felt was the best return for their investment.

It should also be noted that a person's choices may be rational even though the actual choice made may seem irrational, immoral, or frivolous to someone else. In this sense, a derelict choosing to drink the cheapest brand of wine is no less rational than the young attorney who manages to acquire a handsome law library on a small budget.

The two basic concepts of *scarcity* and *rationality* lead us to a third important concept which is called opportunity cost.

OPPORTUNITY COST

Because of scarcity we must make choices and when we make choices we must give up some opportunities to pursue others. When 'A' in the previous example decides to buy the full-size car, 'A' has an opportunity cost of giving up the boat—an opportunity cost of $10,000. In simple terms opportunity costs ask us to consider our next best option.

A discussion and comparison of the salaries of professors in various schools or departments of major universities provides a good example of opportunity cost analysis.

On one level, when I decide to go into law teaching I must weigh the opportunity cost of giving up private practice to teach. I am willing to take less pay teaching in exchange for more control over the projects I work on and for flexibility in determining the hours and days in which I do my work.

On a second level, the reason many argue that law school and medical school professors make twice the salary of history professors is that history Ph.D.s have less in the way of alternative job opportunities outside of the university setting. Because job prospects and salaries are less promising in history than in law, the history professor has less opportunity cost in choosing teaching and thus competent history professors can be hired and retained at lower salaries than law professors.

The concept of opportunity costs also plays a role in distinguishing economic profits from accounting profits. Accounting profits are measured by the return you

earn on an investment. For example, if you invest in an
apartment building (become a landlord) you may make
a four percent return on your investment after taking
into account all of your expenses. Such a return would
be your accounting profit. Economic profit, however
considers opportunity costs. That is, if an investor can
put money into a different market, say computer
software instead of rental housing, and if that alternative
investment carried the same risk but returned a fifteen
percent accounting profit, they would have an opportunity cost (economic loss) of eleven percent from invest-
ing in rental housing; even though rental housing returned a four percent profit.

Given similar risks, investors should prefer the
types of investments that return higher accounting profits. This observation means that attempts to regulate
such things as rental housing must be sensitive to more
information than pure accounting profits. For example,
to impose costs on a landlord, that might reduce the
rate of return from fifteen to four percent, may seem
"fair" because it still leaves the investor with an "adequate profit." The problem is that investors might feel
that they are taking an economic loss relative to other
investment opportunities. As a consequence they may
seek to exit the rental housing market even though it
provides them with a four percent return. Alternatively,
they may stay in the rental housing market and attempt
to further reduce their costs by providing fewer services
or lower quality housing in an attempt to indirectly raise
their economic returns. Because both types of profit
are important factors in setting regulatory policy and
predicting the potential consequences of regulation, economic analysis of such issues should take both types of
profit into account.

Some of the concepts discussed so far can be brought together in the visual context of the *Production Possibility Curve (PPC)*.

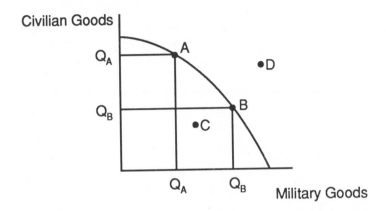

DIAGRAM 1

[F7272]

The classic example of the PPC trade off is to consider the scarcity issue for the U.S. as creating a social choice between expenditures on civilian goods as opposed to military goods. The curve in Diagram 1 shows the limits of our resources at any given time when operating efficiently and thus there is a trade off between civilian and military goods. In order to buy more civilian goods we must give up some military goods and vice versa. We operate efficiently at points along the curve (at points along the curve we are getting the most for our investment).

If we are at point 'C' we are operating inefficiently. Point 'C' represents bureaucratic mismanagement that pays $2,000 for a $.05 cent screw at the Department of Defense. Point 'D' represents an unattainable combination. Point 'D' can only be reached if over time we develop new technologies or resources that make us richer or more productive. This would gradually shift the curve outwards and if the economy expanded enough, we would be able to reach point 'D'.

[Note that this same diagram can be used to represent an individual's choice between spending and saving, with the position of *the curve* being determined by the individual's income and the points along the curve reflecting the trade-off between alternative mixes of goods and services.]

SUBSTITUTE GOODS

In considering scarcity and the need to make choices we need to introduce another idea that is relevant to the rational economic person and that is the notion of substitute goods.

Substitute goods are important in getting the best use of your resources. An example of substitution occurred in many factories in the Northeast during the oil crisis of the 1970's. The dramatic rise in oil prices throughout the 1970's led many companies to switch their factory power plants from oil to natural gas or coal. They substituted one good for another based on changing prices and expectations. The changes were not cost free but were undertaken anyway because of an overall cost savings even after figuring in the cost of substitution. The main point is that the availability of substitutes helps one adjust the particular goods consumed based on changes in relative prices.

CONSTRUCTING THE SIMPLE ECONOMIC MODEL—SUPPLY AND DEMAND

Now we are ready to look at the basic conception and use of a simple economic model. In order to do this we must consider two basic components of such a model—supply and demand.

A. Supply or Cost Curve

The cost or supply curve represents the amount of goods that will be supplied to a market at a given price. It also can be used to illustrate the effect on market behavior when perceived social, psychic or other costs raise the cost of a certain activity.

Five important factors about the Supply (Cost) Curve are:

1) Quantity supplied of a good depends on the price of *that* good.

2) Quantity supplied of a good depends on the prices of *other* goods. This refers to relative price. For example, if the price of soybeans goes up, the supply of corn may go down as farmers begin to shift their production from corn to soybeans.

3) Quantity supplied depends on the costs of factors of production. For example, if law school tuition were to rise significantly, fewer people may decide to attend law school, thus decreasing the supply of attorneys.

4) Quantity supplied depends on the state of technology. (The cheaper it is to produce "chips" the more affordable computers and calculators become.)

5) Quantity supplied depends on the goals of the suppliers. For example, if it is more prestigious or socially acceptable to produce chemicals for health care than war, maybe people will be more willing to supply health care needs.

Do not forget that cost also means cost as we discussed with respect to opportunity costs. That is, as a producer you are confronted with choices of what to produce (you can also choose not to produce at all and merely to invest your money elsewhere). As a consumer you are confronted with choices of what to buy. Remember that not doing anything or merely passive investment is always an option. These choices, as we said, involve a system of scarcity. Thus any choice necessarily forecloses another opportunity and that is the cost.

An important concept in understanding supply is *Marginal Cost.* Marginal cost is the increase in cost required to increase output of some good or service by one unit. Although marginal cost may fall at first, it must eventually rise with increased output because of the law of diminishing returns. An example of the law of diminishing returns is that in the production of oil, although the cost of producing each additional barrel of oil may decrease at first, eventually it will cost more to produce each additional barrel of oil because of additional exploration costs and more expensive drilling to tap deeper wells, etc. Therefore, the supply or cost curve is upward sloping and looks as follows:

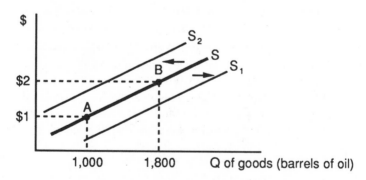

DIAGRAM 2

[F7273]

Going from pt. 'A' to pt. 'B' in Diagram 2 is a movement *along* the supply curve. Movements along the supply curve occur as the price of oil changes. This is called a change in the quantity supplied. Remember the supply curve represents what will be supplied given a certain set of understandings at any given time. A change in the quantity of a good that producers are willing or able to sell that results from a change in an economic condition other than a change in the price of the good itself results in a shift of the supply curve, from 'S' to say 'S_1' or 'S_2'. This is called a change in supply. Note that a shift to the right means that more will be supplied at every price and a shift to the left means that less will be supplied at every price.

A shift in supply comes about only if a fundamental change takes place such as: (1) technological change—if improved technology decreases production costs, supply will shift to the right; (2) changes in input prices—if input prices become more expensive, supply will shift to the left; (3) changes in the prices of other goods—for example if the price of soybeans goes up while the price of corn stays constant, the supply of corn will shift to the left and likewise if the price of soybeans goes down while the price of corn stays constant, the supply of corn will shift to the right; (4) changes in expectations—if suppliers expect the price of oil to go up in the future, they will be less willing to supply oil to the market now and the supply of oil will shift to the left, and if suppliers expect the price of oil to go down in the future, they will be more willing to supply oil to the market now and the supply of oil will shift to the right.

B. Demand Curve

The demand curve represents the amount of goods that consumers will be willing to buy at any given price.

Six important factors affecting demand are:

1) Quantity demanded of a good depends on the price of *that* good.

2) Quantity demanded of a good depends on the prices of *other* goods. If goods are *substitute goods* (ex. oil and natural gas) then an increase in the price of one will result in an increase in demand for the other and a decrease in the price of one will result in a decrease in demand for the other. If goods are *complementary goods* (ex. gas and automobiles) then an increase in the price of one will result in a decrease in demand for the other and a decrease in the price of one will result in an increase in demand for the other.

3) Quantity demanded varies with the tastes or preferences of the members of society (ex. hula hoops, bell bottoms, etc.).

4) Quantity demanded depends on the level of income of the average household. A poor population spends much of its income on basics, and a rich population not only buys more but buys a different mix of goods and services.

5) Quantity demanded depends on the size of the total population, although just having more people is not sufficient, they must have purchasing power.

6) Quantity demanded depends on the distribution of income among households. Distribution of income affects the market—take for example an oil rich country with high average income but actually all the money is in a few hands. Such a situation results in a different type of product mix than if wealth is more

evenly distributed among the general population.

Thus quantity demanded depends on (and changes with) average income, population, distribution of income, the price of the commodity, and the price of other commodities.

We can set up a demand curve much as we set up a supply curve. The whole demand curve is a representation of the complete relation between quantity demanded and price, other things held constant.

The supply or cost curve involves marginal cost. Now we need to discuss *Marginal Utility*. Marginal utility is the additional utility a person receives from consuming one additional unit of a good. This can best be illustrated by an example.

EXAMPLE: It is a hot sunny day and you are very thirsty. You arrive at a soda stand. Your first glass of Coke is very good and of great value to you. In fact you may be so thirsty that you would be willing to pay $1.00 instead of the asking price of .50 cents. Your second, third and fourth glass of Coke are less and less valuable as you are now cooled down and no longer as thirsty. You may not want another glass even if offered for .25 cents or ½ price.

The Coke example illustrates the principle of diminishing marginal utility and thus the demand curve looks as follows:

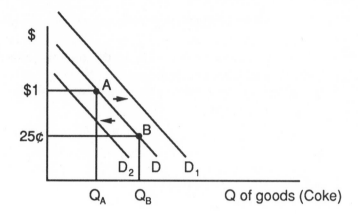

DIAGRAM 3

[F7274]

As illustrated you have a demand curve. At $1.00 per glass few glasses of Coke are sold—maybe only to those who are very thirsty. At .25 cents many more glasses of Coke are sold. This is a movement along the demand curve. Like a supply curve a demand curve can also shift. The causes of shifts of demand curves include:

1) Changes in taste (people decide they like Pepsi more than Coke—so less is sold at every price.);

2) Increases or decreases in population (more or less people to buy Coke or to demand alternative products);

3) Redistribution of income (more people with lower income may prefer water or generic brand cola—or more people with higher income may prefer Perrier.);

4) Changes in average household income (if average household income increases more families could afford Coke.);

5)   Changes in markets of substitute or compli-
mentary goods (change in cost of other colas,
non colas, fruit juices, water, etc. will affect
demand for Coke.).

THE BASIC MODEL

Now we are ready to put the basic economic model
together by combining the concepts of supply and
demand. The basic model serves as a model for general predictions of behavior.

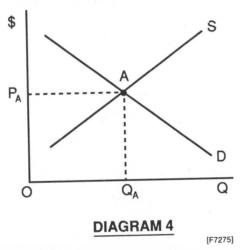

DIAGRAM 4
[F7275]

On this simple diagram the supply and demand
curves intersect at 'A'. For this market, then, 'A' represents a market equilibrium. That is the point at which
marginal cost (MC) equals marginal utility (MU). This
is the point at which all goods supplied are just enough
to meet demand. At prices greater than P_A, sellers will
be willing to supply more than Q_A. Supply will exceed
demand and as sellers' inventories pile up with un-
purchased goods, sellers will cut back on their production. At prices less than P_A, suppliers will be willing to
supply less than Q_A and buyers will wish to purchase

more than Q_A. Additional sellers will enter the market in order to realize the profit that can be made as long as price is greater than marginal cost (which is represented by the supply or cost curve) and the price will be driven down to P_A with Q_A being the resulting quantity sold and purchased. An equilibrium is where there is no tendency for change and therefore a market equilibrium is where the separate plans of the buyers and sellers mesh exactly (quantity supplied = quantity demanded).

Using this simple model, let's take one problem area as an example of how the model might work.

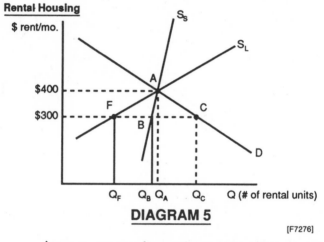

Rental Housing

DIAGRAM 5

[F7276]

Assume we can figure the cost to plan, construct, and operate rental housing. This would give us our supply or cost curve. We also can poll people to find out what they would be willing to pay to rent a given type of apartment. In the above market the efficient or market equilibrium point is at 'A'. This means rent should be $400/mo. in order to fill all the rental units worth filling. Note that the short run supply curve for rental housing (S_S) is fairly vertical. This is because in the short run it is hard for the suppliers of rental housing to be very responsive in terms of quantity supplied to changes in rental income (time and cost of planning and construction make quick and dramatic changes difficult in the short run). In this case, we say that short-run supply is relatively price inelastic.

If the government were to impose rent controls, setting rents artificially at say $300, then in the short run the quantity of rental housing supplied will fall to Q_B, the quantity of rental housing demanded will rise to Q_C, and there will be a shortage of rental housing. In the long run, the rental housing shortage will increase to Q_C minus Q_F as rent controls result in reduced construction or new rental housing. This is represented by a shift in supply from S_S to S_L. If rent controls are set low enough, owners may let their building go without proper maintenance and repair, thus reducing the quality of the rental housing that is available.

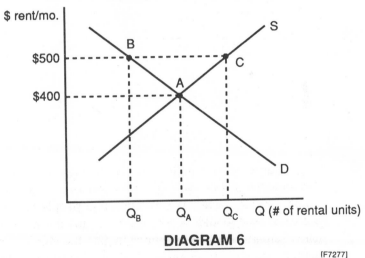

DIAGRAM 6

[F7277]

Diagram 6 illustrates that this same type of analysis can be used to examine the effect on the rental housing market if landlords were to charge more than the equilibrium price. If landlords were to charge say, $500/mo., the quantity of rental housing supplied (Q_C)

would exceed the quantity demanded (Q_B). If landlords actually built a supply up to Q_C they would have to reduce rents or provide bonuses to reduce effective rent in order to get all of their units occupied.

Let's go one step further before we look at some of the assumptions of this model.

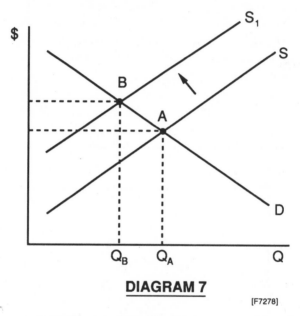

DIAGRAM 7

[F7278]

Consider a first impression court case imposing strict requirements for an implied warranty of habitability on rental housing or a new series of legislation imposing a lot of new duties and obligations on landlords. What result? Increased cost at every point.

Because the legal environment has changed the burden of being a landlord the supply curve shifts to the left and, at any given rate of rent, fewer units will be offered than before. Note how a rent control act that merely sets rent at the previous $400 market rate would now, after the new law and higher rents, be a rent level of market disequilibrium.

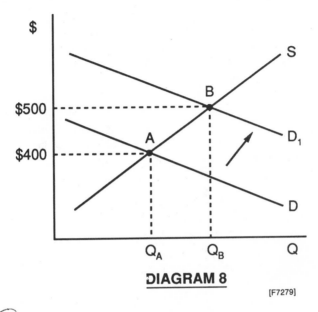

DIAGRAM 8

[F7279]

Suppose, on the other hand, that our original market is not affected by some new set of legal rules for landlords and tenants but rather there is a dramatic change in the cost of home ownership. For example, if housing costs go up and mortgage rates are high, demand for rental units will be higher at every point and thus there will be a shift in the demand curve to the right. This is because rental housing units and home ownership housing units are related. Thus, the prices or activities in one market have an impact on the other market.

ASSUMPTIONS IN ECONOMIC ANALYSIS

Some important assumptions we make with an economic model are:

1) Good information—that individual consumers can get access to a reasonable amount of information;

2) Individuals know what they want and what they want may not be the same as what some outsider or third party governmental agency thinks they should have;

3) Individuals can take clues from the market. For example, if there is a strong demand for rental units, landlords will produce more units. In the time period before production dramatically increases there may be price adjustments upward. In other words, if rental housing returns a good profit from rents based on the cost of producing and running rental units then the market will signal investors to put more money into this product;

4) The market does not care about the issue of fairness or justice. Allocation of scarce resources is made on votes of dollars in the marketplace. The market leaves it to society to provide an equal opportunity for all people to have a chance at success and earning the money to cast their "vote." As long as there are no artificial barriers to success, no one should be offended by the functioning of the market;

5) The economic model we looked at assumed some degree of competition in the sense that there are multiple buyers and sellers. This describes the vast majority of all our activities. (Even in rental housing 70% of the units are run by landlords who are small time owners with only six units or less to rent.);

6) People and resources are freely moveable; and,

7) Acceptance of the current distribution of income and resources. This is important since "economic voting" in the marketplace is based on the current distribution of wealth and this current distribution affects future allocations. The answers generated by a market model approach accept the current distribution of wealth—assumptions about alternative distributions will affect entire supply and demand curves as illustrated in the previous material.

COMPETITION

Competition deserves a little further comment. A common mistake made by many unfamiliar with economics is to draw the wrong conclusion from the simple observation that all sellers are offering similar goods and services for the same basic price. Many people will argue this shows monopoly power or that it shows a market conspiracy. This is not what it proves—you need evidence of another sort to show lack of competition or to show a market conspiracy. Rather, in a competitive market, the market or equilibrium price is set by supply and demand functions for the whole market. If you are one of many suppliers renting apartments, and your units are like hundreds of others already on the market, then your price will basically flow from the market such that in a competitive market prices tend to be similar for similar services. Only to the extent that you can be cheaper than others (an unusual cost savings such as very low cost labor or access to special technology and patents) or distinguish your product from the perceived quality of others can you adust the price. Thus, the observation that all sellers are selling the same basic products for the same basic price and on the same general terms can very easily be evidence of the economist's perfectly competitive market.

While many refinements can be made to this economic model to make it more complicated, further complications do not change the basic nature of what is set out on the preceding pages. Some people say that the assumptions of the basic economic model are too simplistic and unrealistic to be helpful. Regardless of the realistic nature of the model's assumptions, the key test of the model is the extent to which it helps us make predictions about human behavior. At a basic level, the economic approach is validated because it is a useful predictor even if its assumptions leave some room for improvement. The model, for example, accurately predicts consumer behavior when gasoline prices rise from $1.00 per gallon to $5.00 per gallon; consumers drive less, they buy smaller cars, they car pool, etc.

Now that we have examined the components of the basic economic model, we must consider three other fundamental concepts in economic analysis—Coase's Theorem, Pareto and Kaldor–Hicks efficiency, and Arrow's Impossibility Theorem.

COASE'S THEOREM

Activities by consumers and producers often result in externalities. An externality is an adverse (or beneficial) side effect of consumption or production, for which no payment is required (or no payment is received). The emission of pollution as a by-product of a manufacturing facility is an example of an externality. This type of externality can have a negative impact on others. If the neighborhoods surrounding the factory are entitled to clean air and water, the factory owner will have to negotiate with area residents in order to be allowed to

pollute. Similarly if the factory has a right to cause a
certain amount of pollution, residents of the neighborhood will have to negotiate with the factory owner in
order to obtain cleaner air and water. According to
Ronald Coase, society can allocate resources efficiently
even when there are externalities. In order for this to
be accomplished, however, the cost of negotiating must
be nominal. The costs of negotiating are known as
transaction costs and include such things as the costs of
identifying the parties with whom one has to bargain,
the costs of getting together with them, the costs of the
bargaining process itself, and the costs of enforcing any
bargain reached.

Coase's Theorem is best illustrated with an example.[1] Consider a chemical factory whose discharge of
pollutants into a river causes damage to the water
supply of six nearby residents. As a result each resident
suffers $100 in damages for a total of $600. The water
contamination damage can be eliminated in either of
two ways: (1) a water discharge filter can be installed at
the factory, at a cost of $300; or (2) each resident can
be provided with a home water purifier at a cost of $75
per resident for a total cost of $450. In this example
the water discharge filter should be installed at the
factory since it eliminates total damages of $600 at a
cost of only $300. Thus, the cheapest solution to this
externality problem is the efficient economic solution
and it involves abating the pollution in the least cost
manner; by installing the water discharge filter at the
factory rather than having each owner spend $75 for
the collective amount of $450.

---

1. *See* A. Polinsky, AN INTRODUCTION TO LAW AND ECONOM-
ICS 11–14 (For a similar example).

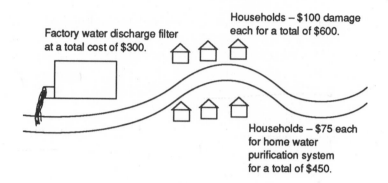

Factory water discharge filter at a total cost of $300.

Households – $100 damage each for a total of $600.

Households – $75 each for home water purification system for a total of $450.

DIAGRAM 9

[F7280]

.   Coase wanted to determine whether the lowest cost alternative would be selected by the parties regardless of the way in which legal rights were assigned. In other words Coase wanted to know if it would make any difference if the right to clean water was assigned to the home owners rather than giving the factory owners the right to pollute. If the law recognized a right to clean water then the factory would have to pay $600 in damages, install a water discharge filter for the factory at $300, or purchase six home water purifiers for the residents at a total cost of $450. In such a situation the rational economic choice would be for the factory to install the water discharge filter. On the other hand, if the law recognized a right in the factory owners to pollute, to operate their factory without having to com- pensate the neighbors for the externalities, then the residents would suffer the cost of the pollution. The residents would have collective damages of $600 which they could suffer or they could correct this by buying six home water purifiers for $450. In the alternative they could get together and buy a water discharge filter for the factory at a cost of $300. In an efficient market the residents would also select the cheapest alternative and would purchase the water discharge filter. As this example illustrates, the cheapest or most efficient method of controlling the externality is reached regardless of the legal allocation of rights, assuming there are zero transaction costs.

Under the assumption of zero transaction costs the most efficient economic alternative is selected without respect to the legal rule chosen, however in the first instance the factory owner had the cost of correcting the problem. This means the factory owner and the purchasers of its product paid for the abatement costs. When the legal rule shifted to allow the factory to pollute, the residents paid the costs. Thus, the legal rule chosen affected which party had to bear the cost of clean water even if it did not affect the choice of clean up method.

Coase then demonstrated that the assumption of no transaction costs is unrealistic. There will be time, inconvenience and actual cost associated with the residents getting together to take collective action and negotiate with the factory. If we assume that for each resident this cost is $80 then we will see that transaction costs may prevent society from attaining efficient outcomes depending upon the selection and allocation of legal rights.

If the rule of law is that residents have a right to clean water then the factory must spend $300 for a water discharge filter, pay damages of $100 to each resident for a total cost of $600 or pay $75 to each resident to buy each person a home water purifier for a total cost of $450. The rational economic decision here is for the factory to purchase its own water discharge filter for $300. Thus, the assumption of transaction costs does not affect the result in our first example because the factory does not have to get together with others to formulate a collective response concerning the residents.

When we decide to impose a legal rule that recognizes the right of the factory to pollute, the result is different. Assuming $80 in transaction costs for the residents to get together, each individual will purchase a home water purifier at $75 rather than incur the cost of $80 each necessary to get together and work out the deal to spend $300 to buy the water discharge filter for the factory. In this example working alone costs each resident $75 whereas working together cost them each $130 ($80 plus ⅙ × $300).

 From this example we see that transaction costs can change the end result of the legal rule selected. Hence, we see that when the factory has a right to pollute, the cheapest method of abating the pollution is not chosen. As a result society spends more of its scarce resources than it should to correct the problem of water pollution. Such an outcome is inefficient from a societal viewpoint but it is economically rational and predictable from the economist's model. Therefore as lawyers, in formulating legal policy, we must be aware of transaction costs and their implications for affecting the efficiency of end state results depending upon the positioning of the legal right in question.

PARETO EFFICIENCY AND THE KALDOR—HICKS THEORY

Economics is constantly concerned with efficiency, or in other words in acting with a minimum of expense, effort, and waste. In discussion of efficiency, the concepts of Pareto superiority or Pareto optimality are often referred to.

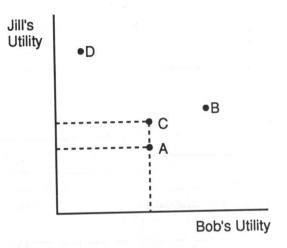

DIAGRAM 10

[F7281]

A change in the status quo is considered to be *Pareto superior* if it makes at least one person better off without making anyone else worse off. For example, in Diagram 10, if point "A" is the status quo, a move to point "B" is Pareto superior because it makes Bob and Jill both better off. Likewise, a move from point "A" to point "C" is also Pareto superior because it makes Jill better off and Bob is no worse off than he was at point "A". However, a move to point "D" is not Pareto superior because although it makes Jill much better off, it makes Bob worse off than he was at point "A". A point is considered to be a Pareto optimum if no more Pareto superior points are available. That is, a Pareto optimum occurs where it is impossible to make any individual better off without making someone else worse off. Pareto optimums are also said to be Pareto efficient. The classic example of a Pareto efficient exchange is a voluntary market exchange where, by definition (in the absence of fraud, duress, or etc.), both parties are made better off, in their own estimation, by virtue of the exchange. They each valued the other thing more than that which they were originally holding or else they would not have made the exchange. In this situation it is easy to see that imperfect information or high transaction costs may prevent otherwise efficient exchanges.

Two British economists, Nicholas Kaldor and John R. Hicks, came up with a different measure of efficiency. The Kaldor–Hicks theory is not concerned with whether or not a reallocation of resources will make certain individuals worse off, but rather with whether or not society's aggregate utility has been maximized. According to the Kaldor–Hicks theory, a reallocation of resources is efficient if those who gain from it obtain enough to fully compensate those who lose from it, although there is no requirement that actual compensation occur.

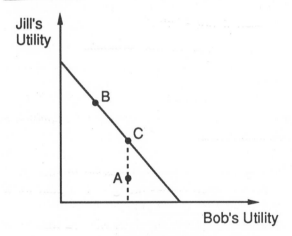

DIAGRAM 11

[F7282]

Diagram 11 can be used to illustrate the Kaldor–Hicks theory. Assume that the diagonal line represents a utility possibility curve for a set amount of resources in society, i.e. points along the diagonal line maximize society's aggregate utility for a given level of resources. A move from point "A" to point "B" is not Pareto superior because Bob is worse off at point "B" than he was at point "A". However, since Bob could be compensated by a move along the diagonal line from point "B" to point "C", which would leave him with the same utility he had before the move, and Jill would still have more utility than she had at point "A", the move is considered to be efficient under the Kaldor–Hicks theory. In other words, the increased benefit to Jill represented by a move from point "A" to point "B" more than offsets the decrease in utility to Bob. As a result, even if Bob is not actually compensated for his lost utility, society is better off in moving to point "B" because there is more total utility as a result of the move than there was before the move. Such a move is, therefore, justified under a Kaldor–Hicks efficiency analysis even if not justified under a Pareto analysis.

An example of the difference between a Pareto superior approach and a Kaldor–Hicks approach can help illustrate the importance of one's choice of efficiency criterion. Assume that Anderson owns a small office building in an urban downtown. The building as used by Anderson is valued at $1 million. The city would like to see a major hotel at the location of Anderson's building as a first step towards an urban revitalization project. Benson comes along with a plan for a major hotel project that if located on the Anderson property would provide the community with $2 million of value. Assume Anderson does not want to sell the property because he values staying in business more than he values getting the fair market value of $1 million for his property. If the city is willing to pay Anderson the fair market value for the property we would not have a Pareto superior transaction since Anderson does not want to voluntarily sell and will have less utility after the

sale. On the other hand, if we used a Kaldor–Hicks
efficiency test we would be able to transfer the property
from Anderson to Benson on the grounds that the
increase in value to the *community* ($2 million) is
sufficient to compensate Anderson for his loss ($1
million) and total social utility would be increased even
if Anderson was made worse off by the transaction. In
such a situation, a Kaldor–Hicks efficiency criterion can
be used to justify a governmental taking of the Anderson property in order to transfer it to Benson as part of
an urban revitalization project whereby the city deter-
mines that the hotel project is important to its economic
redevelopment.   Thus, a Kaldor–Hicks test permits
moves where a Pareto superior test does not. Consequently, when we talk about selecting legal rules that
will promote efficient outcomes it is important to consider the definition of efficiency that is being used.

PUBLIC CHOICE AND ARROW'S IMPOSSI-
BILITY THEOREM

An important and related concept for the use of
economics in law and economics is Arrow's Impossibility Theorem. The Theorem gives us important insight
into the public choice process and into the process of
legislative decision making. This is important if one is
concerned with trying to legislatively implement laws
that promote particular notions of economic efficiency.

Decision making in the public sector can occur in a
number of different ways. Elected government officials
may base their decisions on what they think a majority
of the people want, on what they think the people
should want, or on what they think is most likely to get
them reelected. Kenneth Arrow has done research
(Arrow's Impossibility Theorem) showing that there is
no general rule which can rank social states that is
based only on the way these states are ranked by

individual members of society, which illustrates the difficulty government officials face when they seek to make decisions based on what the majority of their constituents want.

Arrow maintained that four conditions must be satisfied in order for social choices to reflect democratic decision-making (i.e. the preferences of the individuals comprising society). These four conditions are (1) social choices must be transitive (if X is preferred to Y and Y is preferred to Z, Z cannot be preferred to X); (2) social choices must not respond in an opposite direction to changes in individual choice (the fact that some individuals come to like a particular alternative more cannot result in society turning down the alternative if society would otherwise have chosen it); (3) social choices must not be dictated by anyone inside or outside the society; and (4) the social preference between two alternatives must depend only on people's feelings regarding those two alternatives and not on their opinion of other alternatives. Arrow showed that it is impossible not to violate at least some of these alternatives when making a choice among all sets of alternatives.

As an example, suppose the legislature is considering legislation on gun control and must decide between three different options: (1) option A—anyone other than convicted felons can carry guns openly; (2) option B—restricted issuance of gun permits; and (3) option C—total restriction on possession of guns by private citizens. In addition, assume that they wish to do what a majority of their constituents want. The model can be greatly simplified by considering a population of only three individuals. Suppose each individual would rank the options as follows:

PREFERENCES OF THREE INDIVIDUALS FOR ALTERNATIVE POLICIES A, B, AND C

CHOICE	INDIVIDUAL		
	1	2	3
First Choice	A	B	C
Second Choice	B	C	A
Third Choice	C	A	B

DIAGRAM 12

[F7283]

If the individuals first vote between option A and B, a majority (individuals 1 and 3) will vote for option A. If a vote is then taken between options A and C, C will be chosen by a majority (individuals 2 and 3). Therefore, option C would be the final choice. However, if a vote is first taken between options B and C, option B will be chosen, and in a vote between A and B, option A would be the resulting final choice. Similarly, if a vote is first taken between options A and C, option C will be chosen, and a vote between options C and B will result in B being the final choice.

This illustrates that the political process itself (the order in which the options are voted on) is an important determinant of the final choice, and shows how a party or individual that controls the voting procedure may be able to control the result. It also provides a much clearer understanding of the relationship between individual preferences and social choice.

Arrow's Impossibility Theorem, therefore, tells us that we may have difficulty implementing the most socially efficient legal rules. This will be true if those rules are to be based on the collective determination of individual preferences and the legal rules are to be selected through a process of public choice where the process itself is an important determinant of the final outcome. Consequently, the attempt to legislate economically efficient rules must be understood in the context of the problems surrounding the process of public choice. In this sense Arrow's Impossibility Theorem, like Coase's Theory of transaction costs, is an important consideration in any attempt to understand the relationship between law and economics.

CONCLUDING COMMENTS—BASIC ECONOMICS

In this chapter many terms and concepts from economics are explained and illustrated. While this short chapter is no substitute for a long-term study of that complex discipline, it should give the reader a working knowledge of basic terminology and method. Sources (unfootnoted) for much of these introductory comments on economics can be found in the suggested readings that follow.

Suggested Reading

Books

Alchian and Allen, EXCHANGE AND PRODUCTION: COMPE-
TITION, COORDINATION AND CONTROL, (1983 3rd
Ed.).

J. Buchanan, PUBLIC FINANCE IN DEMOCRATIC PROCESS;
FISCAL INSTITUTIONS AND THE INDIVIDUAL CHOICE
(1967).

J. Buchanan, WHAT SHOULD ECONOMISTS DO? (1979).

J. Buchanan & G. Tullock, THE CALCULUS OF CONSENT–
LOGICAL FOUNDATIONS OF CONSTITUTIONAL DEMOC-
RACY (1962).

E. Dolan, BASIC MACROECONOMICS (1983).

M. Friedman, ESSAYS IN POSITIVE ECONOMICS (1953).

J. Galbraith, THE AGE OF UNCERTAINTY: A HISTORY OF
ECONOMIC IDEAS AND THEIR CONSEQUENCES (1977).

F. Glahe and D. Lee, MICROECONOMICS: THEORY AND
APPLICATIONS (1981).

C. Goetz, LAW AND ECONOMICS: CASES AND MATERIALS
(1984).

H. Hazlitt, ECONOMICS IN ONE LESSON (1979).

R. Lipsey and P. Steiner, ECONOMICS. (4th ed. 1975).

H. Manne, THE ECONOMICS OF LEGAL RELATIONSHIPS:
READINGS IN THE THEORY OF PROPERTY RIGHTS
(1975).

E. Mansfield, MICROECONOMICS: THEORY AND APPLICA-
TIONS (1982).

R. McKenzie and G. Tullock, THE NEW WORLD OF
ECONOMICS (1975).

L. Phillips and H. Votey, ECONOMIC ANALYSIS OF PRESS-
ING SOCIAL PROBLEMS (1974).

A. Polinsky, AN INTRODUCTION TO LAW AND ECONOMICS (1983).

P. Wonnacott and R. Wonnacott, ECONOMICS (1979).

Articles

Gjerdingen, *The Politics of the Coase Theorem and its Relationship to Modern Legal Thought,* 35 BUFFALO L.REV. 871 (1986).

Hicks, *The Foundations of Welfare Economics,* 49 ECON.J. 696 (1939).

Kaldor, *Welfare Propositions of Economics and Interpersonal Comparisons of Utility,* 40 ECON.J. 549 (1939).

Chapter Three

IDEOLOGICAL BIAS IN BOTH LEGAL AND ECONOMIC THEORIES

Both economists and lawyers believe in behavioral models.[1] Economists use behavioral models to predict responses to changes in the perceived costs and benefits of engaging in certain activities. In a similar way, lawyers believe that law helps shape human conduct by prescribing or permitting certain activities. A law will yield a predictable response on human behavior (compliance) provided such laws are perceived as normatively good and legitimate. In both an economic and a legal system, social acceptance of either system requires a normative belief that, in its operation and observable consequences upon individuals, the system itself is fair, reasonable, and just. That is to say, members of the community affected by a particular legal system or a particular economic system must believe that the system is legitimate and supportable. In a capitalist free market economy, for example, if a large number of people begin to question the allocation of wealth, the division of profits, and the ownership of scarce resources by private individuals, then such an economic system will tend to be unstable and subject to change. Likewise,

---

1. *See.* Malloy, *Equating Human Rights and Property Rights—The Need for Moral Judgment in an Economic Analysis of Law and Social Policy,* 47 Ohio St.L.J. 163 (1986).

when law and legal institutions become questioned and thought of as illegitimate then those governments and institutions become unstable. Thus, we see, at least in part, explanations for the "socialization" of the economic system in the United States and Western Europe and we likewise see protest and revolution for change in numerous countries such as the Philippines, Chile, China, the Soviet Union and Nicaragua. (The underlying norms and values in each case become subject to question and the status quo becomes subject to change).

It is in this context that we must study both law and economics with particular sensitivity to the ideological bias of any given system of social organization. One may normatively accept and prefer free market capitalism to Marxist communism but one should know that the selection of any one method of social organization by necessity incorporates certain underlying values while rejecting others; this I call ideological bias. The ability to recognize, identify and distinguish or challenge the underlying values and assumptions of a particular view of law or of economics is important for lawyers and legal economists. While it may be rare that an actual American judicial decision reflects any one particular view of the world, it is clear that judicial decisions and legal argument are often times built on underlying assumption which are ideologically based. Thus, the good lawyer needs to be able to decipher hidden ideological bias in legal argumentation so that the most effective case can be made for one's own cause. Importantly, the claim of this book is not that good lawyering is simply a matter of good ideological reasoning but rather that good lawyering requires that a lawyer be able to use these legal and economic arguments as one very important tool, among others, for the presentation of one's position.

Having said all of the foregoing it is now time to say a few specific comments concerning bias in law. Law represents a biased undertaking for several reasons. In the first instance one must acknowledge that the current assignment of legal rights, privileges and obligations has an effect on future rights, privileges and obligations. Consider an example: assume an employer has a private property right to the control and income of her company. If at a later time period the employees assert a right to profit sharing and corporate ownership that assertion will come into direct conflict with the earlier declaration of the employer's private property rights. Furthermore, the community's internalization of the values underlying the rule in favor of the employer will affect the viability of change in the later time period. Given the starting point of legal rules in favor of the employer it will be difficult to move to a new position. Many in the community may not even realize that an alternative ideological view of the "just society" could as easily have started from the proposition that the employees are entitled to ownership and profit sharing from any and all employment. As a result, the likelihood of getting to a position of employee ownership, from a time period that allows the employer to have a private property right in all returns from sales of its products, is less likely than if the starting point reflects a different premise. Consequently, the choice of initial legal rules effects the inertia of change as well as the power to effect change (the employees may have less resources than the employer in this first example) and the normative indoctrination of values within the society.

Another way of viewing this problem might be to say that legal rules find validity in prior hierarchy. That is to say, when capitalist and wealthy individuals are in power it is no surprise that law both confirms and supports this arrangement by providing rules on private property that protect their claims from those of others. Private property rights, even from the perspective of such a free market philosopher as Adam Smith, were primarily seen as rights designed to protect those with property from those without property.[2] In other words, those people that have gained control over valuable resources, have at their disposal the means to more efficiently and effectively influence the law and the legal institutions of a society to their own benefit. Quite frequently, in such a system, the law begins to reflect the values and premises which confirm and legitimize the then current distribution of resources. The important point here is simple: law and legal institutions are not neutral, objective nor predetermined. One can not resolve legal controversies by pretending that the outcomes that are generated by applying apparently neutral general rules are value free.

Like law, economics is a biased undertaking in that the use of any particular economic model embraces specific assumptions and value statements and consequently any outcome generated by the use of such a model will also be biased. One author has put the matter this way:

The study of who gets what and why, unlike the study of plants or planets, cannot help being an ideologically charged undertaking. Despite the laborious techniques and scientific pretention, most brands of economics are covertly ideological. Marxian economics, with its labor theory of value, assumes the inevitability of class conflict, and hence the necessity of class struggle. Keynesianism, with

---

2. *See* Malloy, *Invisible Hand or Sleight of Hand? Adam Smith, Richard Posner, and The Philosophy of Law and Economics,* 36 KAN.L. REV. 209, 223 (1988).

its conviction that industrial capitalism is systemati-
cally unstable, offers an equally "scientific" rationale for government intervention. Neoclassical economics, with its reliance on the efficiency of
markets, is a lavishly embroidered brief for laissez-
faire.[3]

Interpretation of the world around us is often very
contingent and complex, and consequently we find
room in both law and in economics for the "facts" to be
interpreted in more than one way. In the sense that a
particular observer or advocate sees or "colors" the facts
one way rather than another, there is bias towards a
particular ideological view—such bias does not imply an
evil or bad intent it merely indicates that certain inter-
pretations of the "facts" facilitate different ideological
world views. Consider the recurring issue in law and
economics concerning the presence of market competition. Given a simple observation of a few sellers of a
product where each sells substantially similar products
on the same terms and at the same price—is this
evidence of market competition or of market failure?
For the believer in the marketplace these observations
substantiate the presence of a competitive market—a
market where by definition all sellers must take their
price and terms from the market (no seller has the
power to substantially deviate from the market equilibrium). To one more skeptical of the marketplace the
same observations might indicate a market conspiracy
by a few sellers; the complete absence of any meaningful market; or merely serve as proof of the exploitation
of consumers in a world in which they have no bargaining power. As illustrated here, we can see that the
interpretive framework in which we deal can affect the

---

3. Kuttner, *The Poverty of Economics,* ATLANTIC MONTHLY, Feb.
1985, at 74.

way in which we interpret the "facts" around us. Importantly, our views on economic, political, legal and social arrangements will be affected by the way we interpret the "facts." Thus, a given ideological predisposition will lead to a given set of conclusions and consequently will have important implications for law.

The above comments reflect general consideration about the nature of bias in legal and economic thinking. Now let us consider the norms, values, and bias of the more specific matter of the neoclassical economic model. Neoclassical economics is the mainstay of most American economic education and the favorite tool of analysis for scholars engaged in the economic analysis of law. Likewise, it is the focal point of much criticism by those groups such as the members of the Conference on Critical Legal Studies that criticize much of the economic analysis of law by criticizing the neoclassical economic model.

The neoclassical economic model is a model of human behavior based on marketplace analysis using articulations of social costs and benefits.[4] Underlying the neoclassical model are certain assumptions that will be discussed shortly. These assumptions are sometimes attacked as unrealistic, but are defended for their predictive qualities in assessing human behavior. For example, the model may not appear to have realistic assumptions, but if you use it to analyze the impact of a tenfold increase in the price of gasoline it will accurately predict that people will consume less gas than they otherwise would. The real attack on the neoclassical model, therefore, is on the values incorporated into the model,

---

4. *See* Malloy, *Invisible Hand or Sleight of Hand? Adam Smith, Richard Posner, and The Philosophy of Law and Economics,* 36 KAN.L. REV. 209, 242–244 (1988) (The paragraphs concerning the neoclassical model, its assumptions and values, are substantially taken from the above source and are used here with permission of the KANSAS LAW REVIEW).

separate and apart from any discussion of the model's realistic or predictive qualities.

To understand the value structure of the neoclassical model it is necessary to briefly outline some of its major assumptions. First, the model assumes that people act in their own self interest. Second, it assumes, that in the pursuit of self interest, people act rationally. In other words, the rationality assumption is what gives the model its predictive power. Third, the model assumes that people have access to perfect information. This assumption means that people have the knowledge necessary to act rationally in their own self-interest. Fourth, people and resources are assumed to be freely movable. Under this assumption people and resources will follow the uses deemed most valuable by the marketplace. Fifth, the model assumes that there are no artificial restrictions on entry into the marketplace. Under this assumption, the marketplace remains competitive because buyers and sellers are free to move in and out of the market and thereby effectuate the free mobility of people and resources. Sixth, and finally, the current distribution of wealth and resources is taken as a given. Acceptance of the current distribution of income is an important assumption in the neoclassical model because the allocation of resources and rights derived from the model is determined by people casting wealth-based economic votes. In other words, to the extent that people cast their votes in the marketplace by spending dollars, the initial allocation of dollars will affect the outcome of the voting.

Each of the above stated assumptions incorporates certain values. These values need to be stated explicitly. First, because people are able to act rationally to make decisions in their own self interest, it becomes a value to say that they should do so. This value reflects a determination that individuals rather than central planners should make, at least, the vast majority of life's daily decisions. It also presumes that these self-interested choices in the aggregate are an expression of the best choices for society. Second, the notion that people have access to perfect information (or at least reasonably good information) upon which to rationally act implies that there is no economic or educational bias in the ability to process the information. The value expressed here accepts the current distribution of educational and economic resources, leading to disparate results in the processing of information by otherwise equally possessed human beings. Third, the ability to freely move implies a value judgment against the hardship claims of those that fail to uproot their families and relocate. It is a value judgment that dehumanizes the experience of relocating and, therefore, treats the mobility of people in the same indifferent manner as inanimate objects. Fourth, free exit and entry into the market is essential to competition and the results of competition are presumed to be desirable. Fifth, and finally, acceptance of the current allocation of wealth and resources reflects a value judgment in favor of the process by which that allocation came about. It also reflects a value judgment that the current allocation is fair and equitable or at least that there is no fair or equitable means of substantially improving or changing the current situation.

This brief description of the assumptions and values of the neoclassical model is important because it reveals that such a neutral and seemingly objective and scientific model is nonetheless highly value driven. Consequently the results dictated by the use of such an economic method will be biased in favor of the incorporated values. If one rejects the underlying values of the neoclassical model one should likewise have difficulty accepting the validity of its conclusions. In the final analysis both law and economics end up being subjective and value driven undertakings. It is up to the lawyer to unravel these underlying issues and to deal competently with their use in implementing law and resolving difficult issues of social policy.

Suggested Readings

Articles

Baker, *The Ideology of the Economic Analysis of Law,* 5 PHIL. & PUB. AFF. 3 (1975).

Chase, *The Left on Rights: An Introduction,* 62 TEXAS L.REV. 1541 (1984).

Fried, *The Laws of Change: The Cunning of Reason in Moral and Legal History,* 9 J. LEGAL STUD. 335 (1980).

Hayden, *Values, Beliefs, and Attitudes in a Sociotechnical Setting* 22 J. ECON.ISSUES 415 (1988).

Klein, *Of Paradigms and Politics,* 22 J. ECON.ISSUES 435 (1988).

Kuttner, *The Poverty of Economics,* ATLANTIC MONTHLY, Feb. 1985, at 74.

Lanversin, *Land Policy: Is There a Middle Way?,* 3 URBAN LAW & POL'Y 229 (1980).

Malloy, *Equating Human Rights and Property Rights— The Need for Moral Judgment in an Economic Analysis of Law and Social Policy,* 47 OHIO ST.L.J. 163 (1986).

Malloy, *Invisible Hand or Sleight of Hand? Adam Smith, Richard Posner, and the Philosophy of Law and Economics,* 36 KAN.L.REV. 209 (1988).

Malloy, *Is Law and Economics Moral?—Humanistic Economics And A Classical Liberal Critique of Posner's Economic Analysis,* 24 VAL.U.L.REV. ___ (1990).

Malloy, *The Limits of "Science" in Legal Discourse—A Reply to Posner,* 24 VAL.U.L.REV. ___ (1990).

Michelman, *Norms and Normativity in the Economic Theory of Law,* 62 MINN.L.REV. 1015 (1978).

O'Driscoll, *Justice, Efficiency, And the Economic Analysis of Law: A Comment on Fried,* 9 J.LEGAL STUD. 355 (1980).

Schweikhardt, *The Role of Values in Economic Theory and Policy: A Comparison of Frank Knight and John R. Commons,* 22 J.ECON.ISSUES 407 (1988).

Weyrauch, *Book Review, Taboo and Magic in Law,* 25 STAN.L.REV. 782 (1973).

Part Two
COMPARATIVE APPROACHES TO THEORY— AN OVERVIEW

Chapter Four

CONSERVATIVE APPROACHES TO LAW AND ECONOMICS

Conservative theory in the relationship between law and economics is similar to conservatism in other areas of political and philosophical discourse. In the field of law and economics the most prominent conservative is Judge Richard Posner. Conservatives in this field tend to make cost and benefit arguments in support of legal rules that they find to be efficient and against legal rules that they find to be inefficient. In borrowing heavily from the science of economics, the conservative legal economist tends to imply, if not express, that the results of their calculations are scientific—they are seemingly "neutral" and "objective" and free of overt subjective morality. Neutrality and objectivity, however, are not at work here for the reasons pointed out in the earlier chapter on bias in law and in economics. That is, the conservative legal economists tend to rely on one version or another of the neoclassical model of economics, consequently their analysis is biased by the subjective assumptions of that model.

By use of neoclassical economics, the conservatives reduce rights and obligations to numerical calculations and then proceed to balance countervailing claims by means of scientific equations. It is argued that an efficient result will maximize wealth and that wealth maximization produces the best attainable social arrangement. Within the conservative vision of law and economics there is, therefore, no concept of inherent rights of the individual merely as a result of being a human being. Natural rights or inalienable rights are non-existent to the extent that they can not be factored into the cost and benefit analysis methodology.

As a result, conservative theory tells us that individuals that are down on their luck without a job, or poor as a result of no fault of their own, are simply without a legally recognizable claim to any of society's resources. Judge Richard Posner makes this point clear when he describes his own theory of economic efficiency which uses the Kaldor–Hicks efficiency approach and which Posner refers to as "wealth maximization." In his book THE ECONOMICS OF JUSTICE Posner says:

> Another implication of the wealth-maximization approach, however, is that people who lack sufficient earning power to support even a minimum decent standard of living are entitled to no say in the allocation of resources unless they are part of the utility function of someone who has wealth. This conclusion may seem to weigh too heavily the individual's particular endowment of capacities. If he happens to be born feeble-minded and his net social product is negative, he would have no right to the means of support even though there was nothing blameworthy in his inability to support himself.[1]

Elsewhere in the same book Posner goes on to say that under his particular theory of wealth maximization it is possible for slavery to be permissible in an apparent assertion that the proper analysis of slavery is one of efficiency rather than morality.[2] For instance, while

---

1. R. Posner, THE ECONOMICS OF JUSTICE 76 (1983).

2. *Id.* at 86, 102.

others might argue that slavery is wrong simply because it is immoral or because it violates the very
concepts of freedom and of humanity, a conservative
legal economist could argue that those are illegitimate
reasons for being against slavery. Broad questions of
morality, freedom, and humanity are hopelessly subjective. Their response can be that slavery is wrong in
those situations where it is inefficient and it is wrong
precisely because it *is* inefficient and thereby not a
wealth maximizing relationship. In this line of argument slavery would be inefficient because it is a system
of forced labor that provides the workers with little or
no incentive to increase or improve their productivity.
A slave basically gets the same subsistence rewards no
matter how much is produced, consequently the typi-
cal slave has an incentive to do as little as possible.
By comparison to the slave, the worker paid by the
piece or by the hour has incentives to increase productivity. Slavery would be wrong in most cases then
because it is an inefficient method of employing
human capital.

In another passage by Judge Posner in his book
THE ECONOMICS OF JUSTICE he tells us:

> If Nazi Germany wanted to get rid of its Jews, in a
> system of wealth maximization it would have had
> to buy them out. There would be no more eco-
> nomic basis for coercion here than there is in the
> usual (that is, low-transaction-cost) eminent domain
> context.

> But one must not overlook the possibility of
> extending the logic of certain nuisance cases to
> Jews, blacks, and other racial religious, or ethnic
> minorities. If a funeral parlor can depress land
> values, because people living near it are upset to be
> reminded of death, and on this ground can be

condemned as a nuisance, likewise the presence of Jews or blacks in a neighborhood might so upset their neighbors as to depress land values by an amount greater than the members of the minority would be willing to pay to remain in the neighborhood. In these circumstances some form of segregation would be wealth maximizing. The example seems rather far-fetched, however. It is unlikely that ostracism, expulsion, or segregation of a productive group would actually increase a society's wealth.[3]

In these words Posner reveals a key element of the conservative approach to law and economics. The theory itself can justify many actions that the general public might find hard to accept. But even when Posner sees the normative problems with suggesting that the Nazi's should have bought out the Jews or that Jews and Blacks can be treated as a nuisance, he says only that such results are probably unlikely and that the equation of social wealth is unlikely to be improved by eliminating productive groups. In other words, the wealth maximization theory can support these types of outcomes. Within this system of philosophical thought we are forced to counter the possibility of such results by minimizing their probability and by appealing to the offsetting productivity calculations that such groups might be able to contribute; assuming we could agree that they do in fact contribute more than they detract from the community. In any event, a class of feeble-minded people with no resources could not be productive, and their fate, in the Posnerian society, would not be rewritten by appeal to a productivity calculation. Thus, even in the extreme cases of fundamental human rights, the wealth maximization theory looks to a cost

---

3. *Id.* at 84–85.

and benefit analysis in order to determine the appropriateness of any legal action.

In addition to these normative claims about how the law ought to be efficient, the conservative approach of Judge Posner includes a descriptive claim as well. The descriptive claim of conservative law and economics is that the *common law* is in fact efficient. This means that for the most part the rules worked out by the various judges under the common law can be justified as being efficient and consequently wealth-maximizing and socially good. Such a consequence is possible because of the nature of common law adjudication. It can be argued that people with wealth will keep bringing law suits and appealing lower court opinions until they get results that favor or enhance favorable (efficient) outcomes for them. In such a setting there will be a built in mechanism to move the law towards efficient or wealth maximizing outcomes. This is because wealth maximization measures efficiency in terms of people casting their wealth based votes in a neoclassical economic model. The law will end up favoring the wealthy because the wealthy have an incentive to change the law. Furthermore, the law will become efficient when it finally favors the wealthy.

A common charge against this conservative approach to law and economics, is that it is immoral. Such an assertion of course depends upon how one defines morality; the conservative approach defines it within the boundaries of its economic model. Morality is protecting the market model and in promoting efficient (wealth maximizing) outcomes. Another charge against conservative law and economics is that it is indeterminate and therefore subject to political or ideological manipulation despite the outwardly scientific and objective appearance of its methods.

A simple example will illustrate how conservatives can use Posner's theory of wealth maximization to easily manipulate prearranged results and their use of the model, is, therefore, indeterminative and ideological rather than scientific.[4] Consider the question of legalized prostitution and the Posnerian goal of having such pressing social problems answered by the determination of efficient market outcomes; determinations allegedly free of moral influence and superior in claim to any independent consideration of right or wrong. On the one hand, it can be argued that prostitution should be legalized. It represents a voluntary transaction between two consenting adults and, in addition to merely satisfying Kaldor–Hicks efficiency and the wealth maximization principle, it is a pareto superior outcome since both parties are made better off by the exchange. On the other hand, it is just as easy to use the conservative wealth maximization method to include different variables, or to give variables different weights, in order to reach the opposite conclusion. For instance, the negative effects of the availability of prostitutes on the harmony of family life, or the "guesstimation" on increased street crime as a result of prostitution can all be argued to economically and socially offset the value of permitting prostitution. Thus, whether the theory's "scientific" results favor or disfavor prostitution depends on the conservative philosophy used for support. The indeterminacy of such a theory is, therefore, significant because it undercuts the pretensions of the model's ability to generate scientifically "correct" answers to complex social and legal issues. As a result, the key to understanding the value of the conservative theory of

---

4. Malloy, *Invisible Hand or Sleight of Hand? Adam Smith, Richard Posner, And The Philosophy of Law and Economics,* 36 KAN.L.REV. 209, 248–249 (1988) (This example is taken from the above article and used by permission of the KANSAS LAW REVIEW.)

law and economics is the same as to understanding the econometric forecasts for economic growth, inflation, or the price of oil. The outcomes generated by these models are dependent upon and limited to the variables considered and the weight given to each variable. Consequently, when all scientific pretensions are set aside the results of conservative approaches to law and economics are to be found in conservative ideology rather than in the science of mathematical deduction.

Suggested Reading

Books

J. Bennett & T. DiLorenzo, DESTROYING DEMOCRACY: HOW GOVERNMENT FUNDS PARTISAN POLITICS (1985).

A. Kronman & R. Posner, THE ECONOMICS OF CONTRACT LAW (1979).

S. Macedo, THE NEW RIGHT V. THE CONSTITUTION (1986).

R. Posner, ECONOMIC ANALYSIS OF LAW (3d ed. 1986).

Posner, THE ECONOMICS OF JUSTICE (1983).

T. Sowell, CIVIL RIGHTS: RHETORIC OR REALITY? (1984).

G. Stigler, THE CITIZEN AND THE STATE: ESSAYS ON REGULATION (1975).

W. Williams, THE STATE AGAINST BLACKS (1982).

Articles

Baker, *The Ideology of the Economic Analysis of Law,* 5 J. PHIL. & PUB.AFF. 3 (1975).

Baker, *Posner's Privacy Mystery and the Failure of Economic Analysis of Law,* 12 GA.L.REV. 475 (1978).

Buchanan, *Good Economics—Bad Law,* 60 VA.L.REV. 483 (1974).

Carlson, *Reforming the Efficiency Criterion: Comments on Some Recent Suggestions,* 8 CARDOZO L.REV. 39 (1986).

Coleman, *BOOK REVIEW, The Normative Basis of Economics Analysis: A Critical Review of Richard Posner's The Economics of Justice,* 34 STAN.L.REV. 1105 (1982).

Dworkin, *Is Wealth A Value?,* 9 J. LEGAL STUD. 191 (1980).

Kronman, *Wealth Maximization As a Normative Principle,* 9 J. LEGAL STUD. 227 (1980).

Leff, *Economic Analysis of Law: Some Realism About Nominalism,* 60 VA.L.REV. 451 (1974).

Malloy, *Invisible Hand or Sleight of Hand? Adam Smith, Richard Posner, and The Philosophy of Law and Economics,* 36 KAN.L.REV. 209 (1988).

Malloy, *Is Law and Economics Moral?—Humanistic Economics and a Classical Liberal Critique of Posner's Economic Analysis,* 24 VAL.U.L.REV. ___ (1990).

Malloy, *The Limits of "Science" in Legal Discourse—A Reply To Posner,* 24 VAL.U.L.REV. ___ (1990).

Malloy, *The Merits of the Smithian Critique: A Final Word on Smith and Posner,* 36 KAN.L.REV. 266 (1988).

Michelman, *A Comment on Some Uses and Abuses of Economics in Law,* 46 U.CHI.L.REV. 307 (1979).

Posner, *Some Uses and Abuses of Economics in Law,* 46 U.CHI.L.REV. 281 (1979).

Posner, *The Law and Economics Movement,* 77 AM. ECON.REV. 1 (1987).

Posner, *Utilitarianism, Economics, and Legal Theory,* 8 J. LEGAL STUD. 103 (1979).

Posner, *Wealth Maximization Revisited,* 2 NOTRE DAME J.L.ETHICS & PUB.POL'Y 85 (1985).

West, *Authority, Autonomy, and Choice: The Role of Consent in the Moral and Political Visions of Franz Kafka and Richard Posner,* 99 HARV.L.REV. 384 (1985).

Chapter Five

LIBERAL PERSPECTIVES ON LAW AND ECONOMICS

Probably the three most notable writers in the liberal tradition are John Rawls, Ronald Dworkin, and Bruce Ackerman. In providing an introduction to this view of the relationship between law and economics we will focus on the work of Ackerman as an illustration.

Liberal theory in this area tends to reject the conception of an individual's natural or inalienable rights. It is suggested that a conception of natural or inalienable rights is merely a metaphorical road block that stands in the way of progress on social welfare programs. This is because liberals see the appeal to natural and inalienable rights as the mainstay arguments of the people with extensive private property and such appeals are used to protect that property from social reform and involuntary wealth transfers. Liberal theory finds examples of such use in the numerous attempts to block federal government regulation and economic intervention leading up to, including, and following the New Deal. Likewise, liberals point out that much of the libertarian resurgence in private property discourse is focused on the individual's natural right to possess and preserve their private property—the natural output of their time and labor. In this context, liberals view arguments in support of natural rights and inalienable rights as arguments employed by the wealthy to protect

69

their wealth without having to defend their original favored economic position.

Liberal theory, in general, replaces natural rights discourse with a requirement of equality of treatment. In this formulation no individual has any natural or inalienable claim to rights, rather one's rights, claims and duties are contingent upon the political process. Within the political framework, Bruce Ackerman speaks of the liberal statesman and of the need for society to be guided by the liberal statesman. Liberal statesmen engage in an ongoing dialogue in which all actions must be justified. Ackerman refers to this as seeking a *neutral dialogue.*[1] In the context of the neutral dialogue Ackerman seeks to address the problems of power and distribution within society and he attempts to construct an ideological model that will promote the liberal value of equality of treatment while displacing the myths of natural rights and social contract theories of power.[2]

The key elements of Ackerman's neutral dialogue can be briefly set out as follows.[3]

(1) *Rationality.* Whenever anyone in the society questions the distribution of power or resources the person with power must be able to explain why they have more of the desired item than someone else. Engagement in persuasive philosophical dialogue is required.

(2) *Consistency.* The reasons advanced for the justification of a particular unequal distribution of power and resources must be consistent with the reasons given as a justification for other claims to

---

1. See B. Ackerman, SOCIAL JUSTICE IN THE LIBERAL STATE (1980).

2. *Id.* at 1–30.

3. *Id.*

power and resources. The statement that Whites are superior to Blacks would, for instance, be inconsistent with a statement of all people are created equal.

(3) *Neutrality.* No reason is a good reason within this context if it is based on a claim that the superior resource or power holder has a better conception of the social good than others do, nor is it a good reason if one asserts their intrinsic superiority or an appeal to an intangible higher source such as God. Neutrality requires the engagement in persuasive philosophical dialogue to be free of statements that are typically employed by parents against their children. Such as—"that is the way you will do it because I say so," "you can't do that because it is a sin and I know what God wants us to do," "we are right because we are your parents," etc.

The neutral dialogue of the liberal statesman, according to Ackerman, begins with the affirmation of a right to equal shares and to equal treatment with respect to the allocation of scarce resources and the distribution and exercise of power. In the liberal arrangement, the burden of articulating justification is placed squarely upon those people that seek an unequal or inegalitarian distribution of society's resources.

The liberal model, as articulated by Ackerman, is fairly representative of the general approach by liberals in this area. The liberal approach puts a great deal of faith and emphasis on the political process. Since individuals have no natural or inalienable rights there is no inherent restraint on state action. The principle of equality only seeks to have the state treat all people equally provided there is no method of neutral dialogue that can justify unequal treatment in some cases. Thus,

the liberal state can do whatever it wants to the individual. The check on the abuse of power by the state is
the political process itself. One might think of this in
the context of a pluralistic society like the United States
or in terms of a small group or committee with potential
conflicts between various people or ideas. The liberal
state ends up protecting individuals, providing equality,
in part because of a fear that the ability to gang up on
one group today establishes the ability to have the same
power exercised against you in the future. The principle of equality and the constraints of the neutral dialogue are in essence a form of legal and social culture;
"a familiar form of polity—the liberal-democratic welfare state." [4]

In some ways the liberal perspective is similar to
the conservative approach discussed in the earlier chapter. Both views seem to reject the moral imperatives of
the natural rights of individuals. Likewise, each construct seeks to justify the taking of action against the
individual. For the market oriented conservative, the
individual is simply subject to the efficient workings of a
seemingly neutral marketplace. For the liberal, the
individual is subject to the liberal dialogue of the liberal
state. Because the ability to engage in meaningful
liberal dialogue requires certain presumptions about
access to education, information, and power in the first
place it is a theory which suffers from certain biases
similar to those that effect the neoclassical economic
model of the marketplace.

In many ways Ackerman's model of the liberal and
neutral dialogue is merely a theoretical replacement for
the economic marketplace. In liberal discourse we
move from the language of the marketplace to the
language of the political forum. Access to political

---

4. *Id.* at 30.

power becomes a replacement for access to economic power and the internal assumptions of the defined liberal dialogue support and protect the internal generation of outcomes regarding the allocation of social resources.

Suggested Reading

Books

B. Ackerman, SOCIAL JUSTICE IN THE LIBERAL STATE (1980).

B. Ackerman, RECONSTRUCTING AMERICAN LAW (1984).

R. Dworkin, A MATTER OF PRINCIPLE (1985).

R. Dworkin, LAW'S EMPIRE (1986).

R. Dworkin, TAKING RIGHTS SERIOUSLY (1978).

A. Ekrich, THE DECLINE OF AMERICAN LIBERALISM (1967).

J. Gray, LIBERALISM (1986).

J. Rawls, A THEORY OF JUSTICE (1971).

M. Sandel, LIBERALISM AND THE LIMITS OF JUSTICE (1982).

Articles

Ackerman, *Law, Economics, and The Problem of Legal Culture,* 1986 DUKE L.J. 929.

Ackerman, *Law in an Activist State,* 92 YALE L.J. 1083 (1983).

Ackerman, *The Marketplace of Ideas,* 90 YALE L.J. 1131 (1981).

Cotterrell, *Book Review, Liberalism's Empire: Reflections on Ronald Dworkin's Legal Philosophy,* 1987 AM.B.FOUND. Res.J. 509.

Fraser, *Laverne and Shirley Meet the Constitution,* 22 OSGOODE HALL J. 783 (1984).

Freeman & Schlegel, *Sex, Power and Silliness: An Essay on Ackerman's Reconstructing American Law,* 6 CARDOZO L.REV. 847 (1985).

Gjerdingen, *The Politics of the Coase Theorem and its Relationship to Modern Legal Thought,* 35 BUFFALO L.REV. 871 (1986).

Hyde, *Book Review, Is Liberalism Possible?*, 57 N.Y. U.L.Rev. 1031 (1982).

Keating, *Book Review, Justifying Hercules: Ronald Dworkin and The Rule of Law,* 1987 Am.B.Found. Res.J. 525.

Marawetz, *Persons Without History: Liberal Theory and Human Experience,* 66 B.U.L.Rev. 1013 (1986).

McKenna, Wade, & Zannoni, *Keynes, Rawls, Uncertainty, and The Liberal Theory of the State,* 4 Econ. & Phil. 221 (1988).

Peller, *The Politics of Reconstruction,* 98 Harv.L.R. 863 (1985).

Priest, *Book Review, Gossiping About Ideas,* 93 Yale L.J. 1625 (1984).

Rawls, *The Idea of an Overlapping Consensus,* 7 Oxford J.Leg.Stud. 1 (1987).

Schauer, *Lawyers and Lawmaking,* 83 Mich.L.Rev. 1141 (1985).

Waldron, *Theoretical Foundations of Liberalism,* 37 Phil.Q. 127 (1987).

Wright, *Professor Bickel, The Scholarly Tradition, and the Supreme Court,* 84 Harv.L.Rev. 769 (1971).

Yablon, *Book Review, Arguing About Rights,* 85 Mich.L. Rev. 871 (1987).

Chapter Six

LEFT COMMUNITARIAN AND NEO–MARXIST APPROACHES TO LAW AND ECONOMICS

In this chapter discussion focuses on an introduction to Critical Legal Studies (CLS). As with any diverse group of individual scholars, there are multiple viewpoints and disagreements within the Conference on Critical Legal Studies. It is nonetheless a fair assertion that CLS critics generally tend to be left communitarians or neo-marxists in their political and ideological approach. CLS scholarship is in the tradition of critical theory and employs traditional methods of deconstruction and reconstruction in formulating arguments. In this context the CLS scholar puts an emphasis on demonstrating the indeterminancy of the legal systems offered by other schools of thought and in showing that no given system of law is intrinsically inevitable.

As varied as the CLS ranks are today, the founding premise of the movement was powerfully simple and succinct. In 1977, a group of academics gathered at the Harvard Law School to denounce the theoretical underpinnings of American jurisprudence, to wit, Legal Realism, Formalism, Liberalism, "and everything else." This is not to say that CLS began as a negative movement. Far from it, CLS was, and continues to be, committed to shaping a society based on some substantive vision of the human personality, absent the hidden interests and class domination of legal institutions. * * * CLS's broad attack on legal discourse as "itself a form of political domination and a barrier to progressive change" inspired a deluge of radical criticism of the traditional role of law in society.[1]

Critical legal theory posits existing law and institutional structure as being contingent, that is being socially chosen. In this context, they proceed to show the bias in the social choice process—a bias that reflects class struggle and exploitation in a way that parallels a Marxist theory of class struggle in the historical evolution of our political and economic relations. CLS scholars assert that current arrangements are not only contingent but that in addition, the use of law and legal discourse to make these arrangements appear natural is a myth, and more importantly a myth that seeks to legitimize past and present class conflicts and exploitations.

Given the focus on class conflicts and exploitations, it is perhaps understandable that CLS tends to talk in a communitarian sense about altruism as opposed to individualist philosophy. The emphasis is in part centered upon creating a new consciousness about the political choices that can be made and in understanding how the current legal structure is illegitimate in the sense that it seeks to mask this reality. A critical approach seeks to unmask current myths and contends that a more public, caring, and altruistic viewpoint would prevail in a society free of the exploitation, hegemony, and alienation caused by the atomistic con-

---

1. Turley, *The Hitchhiker's Guide to CLS, Unger and Deep Thought*, 81 Nw.U.L.Rev. 593–95 (1987).

straints of our individualist, self interested and capitalistic roots.

An early article by Duncan Kennedy titled *Form and Substance in Private Law Adjudication* deals with the contrast between altruism and individualism.[2] Kennedy asserts that these contradictory conceptions coincide to a large extent with a similar shifting perspective in law concerning the use of *rules* and *standards*. Kennedy argues that rules generally correspond to individualistic philosophies. Rules serve a formalistic function that relieves us of the obligation to confront actual facts or reality. For example, we have certain rules about contract formation and about upholding the right to contract as expressed in the agreement between the parties. Following these formalized rules allows us to uphold contracts without having to contend with possible social problems such as disparity of political and economic power between classes. In contrast to a rules approach, a standards approach would look at the situational facts. Standards are related to altruism and they require us to go beyond the formal rules. In this approach one must ask whether the individuals to the contract really had equality of bargaining power; was their educational, economic, and social position such as to provide a true relational exchange of mutual benefit between both parties, or do our rules of contract law merely legitimize an unfavorable exercise of power evidenced by an unfair or coercive "deal."

An example of a contract unconscionability case might serve to explain not only something about rules vs. standards, and individualism vs. altruism, but also help to distinguish a possible CLS approach from a potential conservative law and economics approach.

---

2. Kennedy, *Form and Substance in Private Law Adjudication,* 89 HARV.L.REV. 1685 (1976).

Consider a situation where a poor uneducated person buys an automobile from a Ford dealer and claims that a particular clause in the form purchase contract is unconscionable, and therefore unenforceable. The conservative law and economics approach would start from a consideration of the rules of contract formation and the need for reliability in contract interpretation so as to make economic transactions predictable and efficient. In an economic sense an inquiry would be made concerning the nature of competition in the marketplace. By definition a competitive market provides consumers with the goods and services, including contract terms, that they desire (that they are willing to pay for). If a seller is not providing the consumer with what they want the consumer will simply go to another seller. Even if there is only one seller in the market we still must consider this fact. As long as there are no artificial barriers to entry the consumer is still protected. That is, as long as another seller *could* enter the market there will be new sellers and new contract terms if consumers desire (are willing to pay for) such new terms. Likewise, evidence of multiple sellers in the market with each seller using the exact same contract terms does not prove lack of competition. In a truly competitive market all sellers take their price and terms from the market, no one seller has the power to effectively extract more for the same product. From this perspective the complaining customer would have to demonstrate serious market malfunctions before the claim of unconscionability could be legitimized. The rules of contract formation, freedom of contract, and upholding the bargain between the parties would generally allow one to gloss over particular situational facts. At the same time this approach allows the decision maker to assert that the outcome is dictated not by his or her own morality but rather as the natural conse-

Malloy–Laws & Econ.Misc.—4

quence of rules and theories which promote the efficient attainment of the public good.

In contrast to this conservative law and economics approach a CLS perspective would shift to another frame of reference. A critic would first realize that the current rules of contract law and of theoretical market competition are not predetermined, rather they are the product of social choice. An analysis of these rules would reveal that they are the historical products of a context of class conflict and exploitation. The rules of contract law inevitably favor those that have something (ample wealth and resources) to bargain about. They are rules that formalize and legitimize the possession and transfer of property and wealth and their efficiency and desirability are measured in terms of the enhancement of those already empowered with an overabundant share of society's scarce resources. In other words, the conservative approach encourages efficient outcomes in terms of market definitions and the market measures efficiency by having goods and services move to the parties willing *and able* to pay the most. The legitimizing reference point is one that intrinsically favors the current unequal distribution of wealth and contains within it the very mechanisms for continued class conflict and exploitation. Thus, in our contract unconscionability situation the CLS decision maker would more likely be persuaded by facts concerning the consumer's low level of education, their poor grasp of English, their employment status, and their history of dealing with authority figures, rather than in hearing about the formalistic application of rules in a theoretically competitive marketplace. As CLS scholar, Mark Kelman, tells us:

> * * * one can deny that one's attitudes about others are painful or contradictory if one believes that one has established categorical bases [rules]

for dealing with them, for distinguishing benevolent interaction from exploitative attacks. * * * Rules are associated with distancing and role playing; the bureaucrat need not listen as long as he does his job, gives you your due. No one can demand anything but compliance with present rules; conversation and explanation of one's conduct are avoided, for it is easily ascertained whether one has done all he must, one can shut up those who ask for explanation—a rule's a rule, don't complain to me. Ongoing attempts to reassert the coherence and comprehensiveness of doctrine, of whatever web of legal rules purports to describe social relations, are part of a collective effort to pacify and reassure us that we have been delivered from existential tragedy. Rules are the opiate of the masses.[3]

Thus, one sees that the CLS perspective, despite its seemingly internal diversity, is fairly categorized as sharing a generally left communitarian and neo-marxist tradition. And, like conservative and liberal theory it is a perspective that rejects the concept of natural and inalienable rights.

It has been suggested that the critical legal economist, like the Marxist, ironically finds the liberal to be a potentially worse enemy than the conservative. The conservative is easily identified and an ideological attack can be made with ease against the conservative position. On the other hand, it becomes more problematic when a liberal political agenda is at question. The liberal presents the "half a loaf" problem that relieves social pressure for change while basically retaining the original social structure and thereby preventing real social change. Liberal legislation to improve housing quality

---

3. M. Kelman, A GUIDE TO CRITICAL LEGAL STUDIES 63 (1987).

and accessibility for instance, is in some ways worse than doing nothing. The liberal legislation is likely to be underfunded, or inadequately carried out, or compromised to the point that it will do little to alleviate the causes of the problem. In this way liberal legislation can be strongly symbolic even though it may do little to alleviate class conflict and exploitation. But since many people will feel "the job is done", that "housing has been taken care of," the liberal legislative effort may have undercut the momentum for more serious structural change. To the critic seeking a major reordering of power and resources, the liberal statesman might easily undercut the rhetoric and momentum for change by merely prolonging the current social order.

Suggested Reading

Books

K. Boulding, A PRIMER ON SOCIAL DYNAMICS: HISTORY AS DIALETICS AND DEVELOPMENT (1970).

G. Cohen, KARL MARX'S THEORY OF HISTORY: A DEFENCE (1978).

D. Conway, A FAREWELL TO MARX: AN OUTLINE AND APPRAISAL OF HIS THEORIES (1987).

J. Elster, AN INTRODUCTION TO KARL MARX (1986).

M. Kelman, A GUIDE TO CRITICAL LEGAL STUDIES (1987).

C. MacKinnon, TOWARD A FEMINIST THEORY OF THE STATE (1989).

T. Sowell, MARXISM: PHILOSOPHY AND ECONOMICS (1985).

Articles

Bender, *A Lawyer's Primer on Feminist Theory and Tort,* 38 J. LEGAL EDUC. 3 (1988).

Binder, *On Critical Legal Studies As Guerrilla Warfare,* 76 GEO.L.J. 1 (1987).

Chase, *The Left on Rights: An Introduction,* 62 TEX.L. REV. 1541 (1984).

Freeman, *A Critical Legal Look at Corporate Practice,* 37 J.LEGAL EDUC. 315 (1987).

Hutchinson & Monahan, *The "Rights" Stuff: Roberto Unger and Beyond,* 62 TEX.L.REV. 1477 (1984).

Kelman, *Consumption Theory, Production Theory, and Ideology in the Coase Theorem,* 52 S.CAL.L.REV. 669 (1979).

Kennedy, *Cost–Benefit Analysis of Entitlement Problems: A Critique* 33 STAN.L.REV. 387 (1981).

Kennedy, *Freedom and Constraint in Adjudication: A Critical Phenomenology,* 36 J.LEGAL EDUC. 518 (1986).

Kennedy, *Form and Substance in Private Law Adjudication,* 89 HARV.L.REV. 1685 (1976).

Kennedy, *The Stages of Decline of the Public/Private Distinction,* 130 U.PA.L.REV. 1349 (1982).

Kennedy & Klare, *A Bibliography of Critical Legal Studies* 94 YALE L.J. 461 (1984).

Kennedy & Michelman, *Are Property and Contract Efficient,* 8 HOFSTRA L.REV. 711 (1980).

Krygier, *Critical Legal Studies and Social Theory—A Response to Alan Hart,* 7 OXFORD J.LEG.STUD. 26 (1987).

Lubin, *Legal Modernism,* 84 MICH.L.REV. 1656 (1986).

Markovits, *Duncan's Do Nots: Cost–Benefit Analysis and the Determination of Legal Entitlements,* 36 STAN.L.REV. 1169 (1984).

Presser, *Some Realism About Orphism or The Critical Legal Studies Movement and The New Great Chain of Being: An English Legal Academics Guide to the Current State of American Law,* 79 NW U.L.REV. 869 (1985).

Rubin, *Does Law Matter? A Judge's Response to the Critical Legal Studies Movement,* 37 J.LEGAL EDUC. 307 (1987).

Russell, *The Critical Legal Studies Challenge to Contemporary Mainstream Legal Philosophy,* 18 OTTAWA L.REV. 1 (1986).

Schwartz, *With Gun and Camera Through Darkest CLS–Land* 36 STAN L.REV. 413 (1984).

Stick, *Can Nihilism Be Pragmatic?,* 100 HARV.L.REV. 332 (1986).

Stick, *Charting The Development of Critical Legal Studies,* 88 COLUM.L.REV. 407 (1988).

Turley, *The Hitchhiker's Guide to CLS, Unger and Deep Thought,* 81 NW U.L.REV. 593 (1987).

Tushnet, *An Essay on Rights,* 62 TEX.L.REV. 1363 (1984).

Tushnet, *Critical Legal Studies: An Introduction to its Origins and Underpinnings,* 36 J. LEGAL EDUC. 505 (1986).

Tushnet, *Critical Legal Studies and Constitutional Law: An Essay in Deconstruction,* 36 STAN.L.REV. 623 (1984).

Unger, *The Critical Legal Studies Movement,* 96 HARV. L.REV. 561 (1983).

Chapter Seven
LIBERTARIAN CONCEPTIONS OF LAW AND ECONOMICS

Libertarians put a great deal of emphasis on private property and individual rights and they are suspicious of the exercise of state power. They believe that private sources of power must be available to keep the exercise of state power under control and within reasonable boundaries. Libertarians tend to recognize that individuals are the relevant reference point for liberty and they tend to view these individuals as having certain natural rights or certain inalienable rights that vest each person with a sphere of personal autonomy. The libertarian view, like that of classical liberalism, is essentially an anti-statists philosophy and in this regard stands in contrast to the views of conservatives, liberals, left communitarians, and neo-marxists.

Libertarians tend to speak of the state of nature and of the minimal state. The state of nature defines the original framework that gives rise to private ownership. That is, in the original state of nature people freely roam the earth and it is through hard work and individual labor that certain resources such as wild game, trees, or minerals are brought under control and put to use. It is the application of labor and the natural right to the fruits of one's labor that justifies the emerging concepts of private property and of individual rather than state ownership.

It is the recognition of private property rights that is said to create the natural incentives for people to create valuable goods and services and which leads to an environmentally sound allocation of scarce resources. Libertarians, for instance, might argue that the problem of over using certain natural resources, such as air and water, is due to the lack of private property rights in these resources. If air and water could be allocated in a private market there would be a system in place for allocating their use and as demand increased prices would rise and consequently there would be a mechanism for reducing the potential for over use. Of course such a system would mean that the resources of air and water would not be "free" and thus some politically motivated groups would be upset by this. However, these resources are not free anyway, we all pay because of overuse through such unpleasant externalities as pollution and shortages of supply. It is only the appearance of being costless and not the reality of the use without cost that is evident when no private rights are attached to such resources.

A key element of libertarian philosophy is its focus on the conception and role of the state. Libertarians attach a strong moral claim to the foundations of private property and of the free market process for the allocation of private resources. Within this framework they recognize a legitimate role for government within the bounds of something they often refer to as the minimal state.

The libertarian conception of the minimal state is affectively argued by Robert Nozick and basically asserts that the conception or limits of the state are found by reference to the state of nature. This is to say that, in the absence of an organized state, individuals will nonetheless find it beneficial to organize or mutually agree to be bound by obligations for certain services. An example might be to provide for the public defense. Some members of the community would specialize in protecting the group's necessary work and food production from the encroachment of roaming warriors or other villages. That type arrangement, leaving others to tend to the production of goods and services, would be so beneficial that it would naturally arise out of the state of nature. It then becomes the ground for argumentation that such services as public defense and others, that would arise only in the natural order of things, helps define the minimal state and it is this notion of the minimal state that should be translated into the organized state.

Richard Epstein makes a good argument for incorporating a libertarian view of government and of the U.S. Constitution into his recent book, _Takings_.[1]

In _Takings_ Epstein reminds us of a fundamental difference between the libertarian perspective and that of conservative, liberals, left communitarian, and neo-marxists—that difference centers around the belief in natural and inalienable rights.

> * * * [T]he political tradition in which I operate
> * * * rests upon a theory of "natural rights."
> * * * Whatever their differences, at the core all
> theories of natural rights reject the idea that private
> property and personal liberty are solely creations of
> the state, which itself is only other people given
> extraordinary powers. Quite the opposite, a natural rights theory asserts that the end of the state is
> to protect liberty and property, as those conceptions are understood independent of and prior to
> the formation of the state. No rights are justified
> in a normative way simply because the state

1. R. Epstein, TAKINGS: PRIVATE PROPERTY AND THE POWER OF EMINENT DOMAIN (1985).

chooses to protect them, as a matter of grace. To use a common example of personal liberty: the State should prohibit murder because it is wrong; murder is not wrong because the State prohibits it. The same applies to property: trespass is not wrong because the State prohibits it, it is wrong because individuals own private property.[2]

From the libertarian's perspective it is the protection of the individual's property rights which stand in the way of involuntary wealth transfers. A forced transfer of wealth from "A" to "B" is a violation of "A's" rights, assuming that "A" obtained her property in a legitimate way. (Note, a CLS scholar might question the formulation of the legitimate means test as well as the original distribution sought to be preserved). It is for these libertarian reasons that Epstein ends up concluding that everything since Franklin Roosevelt and The New Deal is unconstitutional and contrary to his philosophical vision of the proper relationship between the individual, the community, and the state. The libertarian model of law and economics is very much against using the power of the state against individuals to transfer wealth, whether the transfer is for a "conservative" agenda, of helping U.S. corporations compete better overseas, or for a "liberal agenda", such as helping union members attain protective wage legislation.

The libertarian perspective focuses on the individual and recognizes that there will always be an unequal distribution of wealth and resources so long as there are different individual attributes held by each person. Any attempts to enforce specific end-state distributions will be unsuccessful if individuals are given any opportunities for making allocation decisions themselves. This

---

2. *Id.* at 5–6.

concept holds true even in a socialist society. As long as people are given some chance to engage in voluntary transfers there will be a shifting of wealth away from the planned distribution. Robert Nozick illustrates this point with an example of Wilt Chamberlain.[3] If an equal distribution of pay was forced on all basketball players some basketball players, such as Wilt Chamberlain, would end up with more income if fans could engage in some voluntary wealth transfers. Assume that fans could come to a game and put extra money in a box marked for Wilt, the eventual outcome would be that Wilt would make more money than other players because fans would be willing to pay more to see his special talents. Likewise, with the talents of a special teacher, jeweler, baker, carpenter, and etc. As long as people can direct their own resources it will be impossible to maintain an end-state distribution of equality in the absence of continuous state interference with people's lives. Individuals will always be willing to exchange some of their planned distribution in order to receive something of pleasure from someone else. And as long as voluntary transactions are permitted, those that offer the best or most pleasing goods and services will accumulate the most resources from such exchanges. In this way private property rights are always getting redistributed and there will be no way to maintain equality of distribution or outcome in the absence of continuous state interference that will, by definition, destroy individual liberty and choice.

3. R. Nozick, Anarchy, State, and Utopia 162–164 (1974).

Suggested Reading

Books

D. Deleon, THE AMERICAN AS ANARCHIST: REFLECTIONS ON INDIGENOUS RADICALISM (1978).

R. Epstein, TAKINGS: PRIVATE PROPERTY AND THE POWER OF EMINENT DOMAIN (1985).

FREEDOM AND VIRTUE—THE CONSERVATIVE/LIBERTARIAN DEBATE (G. Carey ed. 1984).

FREEDOM, FEMINISM, AND THE STATE (W. McElroy ed. 1982).

R. Lane, THE DISCOVERY OF FREEDOM: MAN'S STRUGGLE AGAINST AUTHORITY (1984).

A. Nock, OUR ENEMY, THE STATE (1983).

R. Nozick, ANARCHY, STATE, AND UTOPIA (1974).

E. Paul, EQUITY AND GENDER: THE COMPARABLE WORTH DEBATE (1989).

M. Rothbard, FOR A NEW LIBERTY: THE LIBERTARIAN MANIFESTO (1978).

M. Rothbard, MAN, ECONOMY, AND STATE; A TREATISE ON ECONOMIC PRINCIPLES (1970).

J. Tuccille, RADICAL LIBERTARIANISM; A NEW POLITICAL ALTERNATIVE (1970).

Articles

Alexander, *Takings of Property and Constitutional Serendipity,* 40 U.MIAMI L.REV. 223 (1986).

Barry, *The Classical Theory of Law,* 73 CORNELL L.REV. 283 (1988).

Ellickson, *Adverse Possession and Perpetuities Law: Two Dents in the Libertarian Model of Property Rights,* 64 WASH.U.L.Q. 723 (1986).

Epstein, *Past and Future: The Temporal Dimension in The Law of Property* 64 WASH.U.L.Q. 667 (1986).

Epstein, *The Classical Legal Tradition,* 73 CORNELL L.REV. 292 (1988).

Epstein, *The Fundamentals of Freedom of Speech,* 10 HARV.J.L. & PUB.POL'Y 53 (1987).

Epstein, *Why Restrain Alienation?,* 85 COLUM.L.REV. 970 (1985).

Grey, *The Malthusian Constitution,* 41 U.MIAMI L.REV. 21 (1986).

Mikva, *Government, Society, and Anarchy,* 38 MERCER L.REV. 753 (1987).

Paul, *A Reflection on Epstein and His Critics,* 41 U.MIAMI L.REV. 235 (1986).

Paul, *Book Review, Searching For The Status Quo,* 7 CARDOZO L.R. 743 (1986).

Peller, *The Classical Theory of Law,* 73 CORNELL L.REV. 300 (1988).

Radin, *The Consequences of Conceptualism,* 41 U.MIAMI L.REV. 239 (1986).

Rhoden, *The Limits of Liberty: Deinstitutionalization, Homelessness, and Libertarian Theory,* 31 EMORY L.J. 375 (1982).

Sax, *Book Review, Takings,* 53 U.CHI.L.REV. 279 (1986).

Sunstein, *Two Faces of Liberalism,* 41 U.MIAMI L.REV. 245 (1986).

Chapter Eight

CLASSICAL LIBERAL THEORY AND LAW AND ECONOMICS

Classical liberalism is like libertarianism in its focus on the individual and in its belief in natural and inalienable rights. In addition, it seeks a process of public and private balance for the purpose of ensuring individual liberty. That is, it seeks to protect individuals from the coercive power of other individuals, groups, or organizations in society by giving coercive power to a democratic state. At the same time it is suspicious and fearful of the potential to abuse the power of the *state* and consequently seeks to preserve private sources of power through the means of capitalism. It is from the give and take of counterbalancing public (state) and private (capitalist) power sources that the classical liberal believes the broadest base of people and ideas will be allowed to coexist in society. For the classical liberal, the neoclassical economic model serves as a metaphor for the proper balance and relationship that should exist between individuals, the community, and the state. The market model, as such, does not hold any special power in terms of providing socially "correct" answers. The market model provides a framework for discussing relationships but, ultimately, questions of individual liberty and human dignity are moral questions which require normative analysis independent from the confines and assumptions of neoclassical economics. As contrasted with conservative theory, for instance, classical liberals know that slavery is wrong, not because it is inefficient, but because slavery violates human dignity and destroys the essence of individual liberty.

Classical liberals find support for their views in the work of Adam Smith and in his dualistic conception of individual liberty and human dignity. This means they believe in both a non-relative and a relative aspect of natural rights. Every person has a *non-relative* (never changing) right to be treated fairly and equally under a system of justice. Every person also has a *relative* right that requires the claims of human dignity to be analyzed in material terms according to the social, economic, and historical context in question. The requirements of human dignity in this model, mean that one must always evaluate social welfare claims in a historical context and cannot merely dismiss or legitimize the personal tragedies and hardships of individuals by cloaking them in the language of efficiency and wealth maximization. In classical liberal theory the marketplace is merely a means to another end, individual liberty, and it is not an end in itself. In this context, classical liberalism is also unconstrained by the libertarian search for the minimal state. Instead, the classical liberal seeks to define a state that serves as an appropriate counterbalance to private coercion. This may or may not be the minimal state of nature depending upon the economic, political, social and historical context in question. It is the idea of competing power sources and decentralized decision making that is crucial to classical liberal theory rather than the definition of a minimal state independent of current cultural understanding.

By following the philosophy of Adam Smith, classical liberals recognize the need for moral judgment in the assessment of law and social policy in order to protect individual liberty.[1] In pursuing the protection of individual liberty through social cooperation, the classical liberal is willing to restrain certain individual conduct by implementation of general rules through a process which respects the human dignity of each person. Furthermore, the classical liberal envisions an affirmative role for government action when there is a significant social purpose involved; such as the protection of basic human dignity by providing food, shelter, medical care and education; and when the private market is unlikely to provide these goods and services without government intervention; such as when the intended recipients are poor and have no purchasing power by which to command the attention of private suppliers.

Classical liberalism is a philosophy that does not believe in capitalism or the free market for their own sake. Rather, it is a philosophy that puts paramount value on freedom and individual liberty as the ultimate objective, with capitalism and the free market identified as the best means for achieving and maintaining that objective. Consequently, all law and social policy claims that seek justification on the basis of prior or current political and economic arrangements, or which are based on the renditions of neoclassical economic analysis, are subject to continuing critical review in light of the moral imperative to protect and advance freedom and individual liberty within a classical liberal framework.

In classical liberal philosophy, concerns for economic efficiency are distinctly secondary to concerns for freedom and individual liberty. Milton Friedman, a

---

1. *See* Malloy, *Invisible Hand or Sleight of Hand? Adam Smith, Richard Posner, and the Philosophy of Law and Economics,* 36 KAN.L. REV. 209, 255–257 (1988) (From here to the end of the chapter the material is taken from the above article and used by permission of the KANSAS LAW REVIEW.)

longtime spokesperson for classical liberal philosophy, has expressed this very opinion for years. As long ago as 1962, when his book CAPITALISM AND FREEDOM was first published, Friedman argued that capitalism was a necessary but not a sufficient basis for freedom. In other words, capitalism could not be the ultimate objective because capitalism itself does not assure freedom. More recently, in a 1987 article, Friedman said:

> A free society, I believe, is a more productive society than any other; it releases the energies of people, enables resources to be used more effectively and enables people to have a better life. But that is not why I am in favor of a free society. I believe and hope that I would favor a free society even if it were less productive than some alternative—say, a slave society.
>
> I favor a free society because my basic value is freedom itself.[2]

These views, expressed by Friedman, are consistent with the views of another great contemporary classical liberal philosopher, Friedrich Hayek,

Hayek, like Friedman, seeks to protect individual liberty from the coercive interference of others, including the state. For Hayek, spontaneous social order, (social order without central government planning), is only possible in the capitalist society and therefore capitalism allows for the greatest sphere of individual autonomy. He believes in the free marketplace and in a maximum of individual autonomy but also acknowledges that the expression of freedom sometimes requires the government to act to protect basic liberties. Such action is permitted if it proceeds by general rules

---

2. Friedman, *Free Market and Free Speech*, 10 HARV.J.L. & PUB. POL'Y 1, 7 (1987).

and is otherwise consistent with concerns for human dignity and liberty.

Summary   In classical liberal theory, therefore, economics provides a tool and a guide to critical evaluation of law and social policy. It provides a means for analyzing alternative approaches to social policy that enhance ordinary legal analysis. The economic model, however, is no substitute for individual moral judgment. The classical liberal does not delegate or obscure difficult moral questions with simplistic and formalistic concepts such as wealth maximization. Rather, the classical liberal engages in an ongoing dialogue designed to further freedom by offering the concept of individual liberty and human dignity as the bedrock values of social cooperation. Furthermore, through this dialogue, classical liberals seek to influence and establish the general rules of social morality, which are as Adam Smith said, "ultimately founded upon experience of what, in particular instances, our moral faculties, our natural sense of merit and propriety, approve or disapprove of." In this way, moral judgment remains an important part of the classical liberal theory of law and economics, and classical liberal philosophy provides a constructive basis for aiding lawyers in the process of social evolution.

Classical liberals for example, are able to support many government programs such as a guaranteed minimum income, public education, job training, and housing. Their methods for achieving these goals, once the moral objective has been determined, would be consistent with information provided by economic analysis. That is to say, for instance, that a concern for providing an adequate supply of low-income housing would not lead the classical liberal to suggest such economically destructive policies as rent control or the direct construction of so-called "public housing." To the contrary, rent control would be rejected on the grounds that basic economic analysis reveals that it hurts rather than helps the poor by discouraging the production of rental housing stock. Likewise, public housing in the form of government controlled "projects" would be rejected for the reason that a government monopoly of low-income housing would be less beneficial to the poor than housing vouchers that could be used by tenants to shop the market for reasonable housing. In this way the classical liberal attempts to blend moral judgment and normative social values with the powerful analytical tools of economics. But, economic models can not be treated as "god like" creatures and they must ultimately be subject to a principled analysis of what it means to be a human being, and it is precisely this question which requires us to consider Adam Smith's dualistic conception of individual liberty. While neoclassical economic methods can help us analyze the consequences or impacts of alternative approaches to resolving pressing social problems they cannot tell us what relative rights an individual is entitled to—healthcare, housing, a job, etc. Fundamental questions of what it means to be a person and to participate in a given community are not answered by neoclassical economic methods, instead they must be answered by an ongoing social dialogue; a dialogue that for the classical liberal is to take place within the framework of classical liberal philosophy on the relationship, between the individual, the community, and the state.

Suggested Reading

Books

M. Friedman, BRIGHT PROMISES, DISMAL PERFORMANCE: AN ECONOMIST'S PROTEST (W. Allen ed. 1983).

M. Friedman, CAPITALISM AND FREEDOM (1962 reissued 1982).

M. Friedman & R. Friedman, FREE TO CHOOSE: A PERSONAL STATEMENT (1980).

M. Friedman & R. Friedman, TYRANNY OF THE STATUS QUO (1984).

F. Hayek, LAW, LEGISLATION AND LIBERTY—RULES AND ORDER (1973).

F. Hayek, LAW, LEGISLATION AND LIBERTY—THE MIRAGE OF SOCIAL JUSTICE (1976).

F. Hayek, LAW, LEGISLATION AND LIBERTY—THE POLITICAL ORDER OF A FREE PEOPLE (1979).

F. Hayek, THE CONSTITUTION OF LIBERTY (1960).

F. Hayek, THE COUNTER-REVOLUTION OF SCIENCE: STUDIES ON THE ABUSE OF REASON (1952).

F. Hayek, THE FATAL CONCEIT: THE ERRORS OF SOCIALISM (1989).

F. Hayek, THE ROAD TO SERFDOM (1944).

LAW AND ENLIGHTENMENT IN BRITAIN (T. Campbell & N. MacCormack, ed. 1990. *See* Chapter by Malloy, *Adam Smith's Conception of Individual Liberty*).

III. LAW AND SEMIOTICS (R. Kevelson, Ed.1989. *See* chapter by Malloy, *of Icons, Metaphors, and Private Property —The Recognition of "Welfare" Claims in the Philosophy of Adam Smith*).

R. Malloy, PLANNING FOR SERFDOM: A CONTEXTUAL THE-
ORY OF LAW, ECONOMICS, AND THE STATE (forthcoming, from the Univ. of Penn Press, 1990).

Articles

Barry, *The Classical Theory of Law,* 73 CORNELL L.REV.
783 (1988).

Epstein, *The Classical Legal Tradition,* 73 CORNELL
L.REV. 292 (1988).

Friedman, *Free Markets and Free Speech* 10 HARV.J.L.
& PUB.POL'Y 1 (1987).

Gray, *F.A. Hayek and The Rebirth of Classical Liberalism,* 5 LITERATURE OF LIBERTY 19 (1982).

Hoeflich & Malloy, *The Shattered Dream of American
Housing Policy—The Need for Reform,* 26 B.C.L.
REV. 655 (1985).

Malloy, *Equating Human Rights and Property Rights—
The Need for Moral Judgment in an Economic
Analysis of Law and Social Policy,* 47 OHIO ST.L.J.
163 (1986).

Malloy, *Invisible Hand or Sleight of Hand? Adam
Smith, Richard Posner, and the Philosophy of Law
and Economics,* 36 KAN.L.REV. 209 (1988).

Malloy, *Is Law and Economics Moral?—Humanistic
Economics and a Classical Liberal Critique of Posner's Economic Analysis,* 24 VAL.U.L.REV. ___
(1990).

Malloy, *Market Philosophy in the Legal Tension Between Children's Autonomy and Parental Authority,* 21 IND.L.REV. 889 (1988).

Malloy, *The Economics of Rent Control—A Texas Perspective,* 17 TEX.TECH.L.REV. 797 (1986).

Malloy, *The Limits of "Science" in Legal Discourse—A
Reply to Posner,* 24 VAL.U.L.REV. ___ (1990).

Malloy, *The Merits of The Smithian Critique: A Final Word on Smith and Posner,* 36 KAN.L.REV. 266 (1988).

Malloy, *The Political Economy of Co-Financing America's Urban Renaissance,* 40 VAND.L.REV. 67 (1987).

Peller, *The Classical Theory of Law,* 73 CORNELL L.REV. 300 (1988).

*

Part Three

PRACTICAL APPLICATIONS— A LOOK AT LEADING CASES

Chapter Nine

CONTRACT LAW: THE ISSUE OF UNCONSCIONABILITY

WILLIAMS v. WALKER–THOMAS FURNITURE CO.

United States Court of Appeals, District of Columbia Circuit, 1965.
350 F.2d 445.

J. SKELLY WRIGHT, CIRCUIT JUDGE: Appellee, Walker–Thomas Furniture Company, operates a retail furniture store in the District of Columbia. During the period from 1957 to 1962 each appellant in these cases purchased a number of household items from Walker–Thomas, for which payment was to be made in installments. The terms of each purchase were contained in a printed form contract which set forth the value of the purchased item and purported to lease the item to appellant for a stipulated monthly rent payment. The contract then provided, in substance, that title would remain in Walker–Thomas until the total of all the monthly payments made equaled the stated value of the item, at which time appellants could take title. In the event of a default in the payment of any monthly installment, Walker–Thomas could repossess the item.

The contract further provided that "the amount of each periodical installment payment to be made by [purchaser] to the Company under this present lease shall be inclusive of and not in addition to the amount of each installment payment to be made by [purchaser] under such prior leases, bills or accounts; *and all payments now and hereafter made by [purchaser] shall be credited pro rata on all outstanding leases, bills and accounts* due the Company by [purchaser] at the time each such payment is made." (Emphasis added.) The effect of this rather obscure provision was to keep a balance due on every item purchased until the balance due on all items, whenever purchased, was liquidated. As a result, the debt incurred at the time of purchase of each item was secured by the right to repossess all the items previously purchased by the same purchaser, and each new item purchased automatically became subject to a security interest arising out of the previous dealings.

* * * on April 17, 1962, appellant Williams bought a stereo set of stated value of $514.95.[1] She defaulted shortly thereafter, and appellee sought to replevy all the items purchased since December, 1957. The Court of General Sessions granted judgment for appellee. The District of Columbia Court of Appeals affirmed, and we granted appellants' motion for leave to appeal to this court.

Appellants' principal contention, rejected by both the trial and the appellate courts below, is that these contracts, or at least some of them, are unconscionable and, hence, not enforceable.

Unconscionability has generally been recognized to include an absence of meaningful choice on the part of one of the parties together with contract terms which are unreasonably favorable to the other party. Whether a meaningful choice is present in a particular case can

---

1. At the time of this purchase her account showed a balance of $164.00 still owing from her prior purchases. The total of all the purchases made over the years in question came to $1,800.00. The total payments amounted to $1,400.00.

only be determined by consideration of all the circumstances surrounding the transaction. In many cases the meaningfulness of the choice is negated by a gross inequality of bargaining power. The manner in which the contract was entered is also relevant to this consideration. Did each party to the contract, considering his obvious education or lack of it, have a reasonable opportunity to understand the terms of the contract, or were the important terms hidden in a maze of fine print and minimized by deceptive sales practices? Ordinarily, one who signs an agreement without full knowledge of its terms might be held to assume the risk that he has entered a one-sided bargain. But when a party of little bargaining power, and hence little real choice, signs a commercially unreasonable contract with little or no knowledge of its terms, it is hardly likely that his consent, or even an objective manifestation of his consent, was ever given to all the terms. In such a case the usual rule that the terms of the agreement are not to be questioned should be abandoned and the court should consider whether the terms of the contract are so unfair that enforcement should be withheld.

In determining reasonableness or fairness, the primary concern must be with the terms of the contract considered in light of the circumstances existing when the contract was made.

Because the trial court and the appellate court did not feel that enforcement could be refused, no findings were made on the possible unconscionability of the contracts in these cases. Since the record is not sufficient for our deciding the issue as a matter of law, the cases must be remanded to the trial court for further proceedings.

So ordered.

DANAHER, CIRCUIT JUDGE (dissenting):

My view is thus summed up by an able court which made no finding that there had actually been sharp practice. Rather the appellant seems to have known precisely where she stood.

There are many aspects of public policy here involved. What is a luxury to some may seem an outright necessity to others. Is public oversight to be required of the expenditures of relief funds? A washing machine, e.g., in the hands of a relief client might become a fruitful source of income. Many relief clients may well need credit, and certain business establishments will take long chances on the sale of items, expecting their pricing policies will afford a degree of protection commensurate with the risk.

The *Williams v. Walker-Thomas Furniture Co.* case was a landmark decision for consumer protection. The majority decision by well known jurist Skelly Wright made great headway for the cause of relief from contract obligations under the doctrine of unconscionability. The major doctrinal question of the case involved the sanctity of upholding a contract as signed by the parties in contrast with disallowing specific terms of the agreement on the grounds that such terms are unconscionable, or in essence not part of what was truly bargained for and agreed to. (The unconscionable term is one that is so one sided and abusive that to enforce it would shock the conscience of ordinary people.)

The *Walker-Thomas* case raises many issues and questions and is in part understandable in an ideological context. Before we consider the ideological issues reflected in Judge Wright's opinion it is useful to discuss the economic implications of the outcome.

Judge Wright was concerned with the credit terms offered to low-income consumers by the Walker-Thomas Furniture Company. By the terms of the credit agreement Walker-Thomas kept an ownership interest in every item a consumer purchased from the store for so long as any balance remained on any item. In other words, no ownership passed to the consumer until all items were fully paid for. Under this credit arrangement a consumer might buy a table for $100 and later buy a chair for $50. After paying a total of $140 the consumer would still own nothing. Furthermore if, at the time a total of $140 had been paid, the consumer bought a T.V. for $300 this would extend the balance due. Thus, the consumer could pay yet another $290 and still not own the original table, chair, or T.V. This was undoubtedly an arrangement that was favorable to the seller, but, was it necessarily unfavorable to the consumer?

Walker-Thomas was selling merchandise to high credit risk customers, people living on low-income, fixed income, and welfare payments. These customers were known to be higher credit risks than upper income employed people. Sellers willing to sell to this high risk customer base had three basic ways to deal with the higher risk of doing business—(1) charge higher prices for the goods; (2) charge high interest rates for credit (usury limits put a legal cap on this alternative); or (3) set up alternative credit arrangements such as that used by Walker-Thomas. In terms of a rational business practice, Walker-Thomas was merely indicating that it needed a higher rate of return to engage in a riskier than normal merchandising operation. This is no different than the demands of consumers when they invest their hard earned savings—they will accept a lower interest rate on their fully insured pass book account than they will for a high risk (uninsured) stock investment.

To do a proper analysis of Walker-Thomas' credit practices and to see if there is a market problem present one needs evidence of the credit terms, prices, and interest rates charged by comparable merchants to low-income, high risk, customers. Evidence that Walker-Thomas was earning higher paper returns compared to stores dealing with lower risk, middle class, customers would be of little value. Comparative evidence is needed with respect to similar risk activities. Only if Walker-Thomas was earning more or dealing on terms far more favorable to itself than similarly situated sellers would we have any evidence of market power—that is the power to dictate terms to consumers as is the case in the absence of a competitive marketplace. The court opinion never addresses this type of analysis.

In holding that credit terms, such as those offered by Walker-Thomas, were unconscionable the court changes the entire market structure. Now, if Walker-Thomas is to serve high risk customers it cannot offset its high risk by credit terms favorable to itself and it cannot charge higher interest rates than those legally imposed by usury laws. In addition, it cannot expect to cover everything by merely charging higher prices because these low-income customers need to buy on credit precisely because they lack the ability to pay on cash terms. Thus, sellers like Walker-Thomas can either go out of business, redesign their business to serve lower risk customers, or find ways to subsidize the high risk customers by passing costs on to lower risk customers.

High risk customers might be subsidized by charging higher prices and having slightly more expensive credit terms for all customers, thus lower risk customers subsidize higher risk customers. This of course can be only partially effective in a reasonably competitive market because low risk customers will shift their purchases to sellers that do not wish to subsidize high risk customers. The only way to avoid this outcome is to use legal means to eliminate competition in the marketplace and require that all merchants make credit available on the same terms to both high and low-income customers.

Instead of considering these and other economic factors, Judge Wright tells us to focus on the respective bargaining power of the parties, their educational achievement levels, their opportunity to understand the "hidden" terms of the contract, etc. In other words, Judge Wright asks us to consider the status of the parties to the contract and the context in which the bargain was struck as opposed to the formalities of finding an executed written contract that we might presume to be the product of free minds in a free market. In taking this analytical approach to the case Judge Wright makes certain ideological assumptions. The assumptions that underlie the opinion in this case are important to understanding the case and they reveal how important it is for a lawyer to structure arguments in the "proper" ideological framework.

Judge Wright's opinion can only be rationalized on an assumption that many of the theories of a competitive marketplace are incorrect. Either the benefits of market competition are completely mythical or at least there is no competitive market operating here. The opinion does not emphasize evidence of no competitive market nor does it seek to define the market. It therefore assumes that people of a certain status—poor, uneducated, high credit risks, predominantly Black—are exploited by whatever market mechanism is at work in the Washington, D.C. environment. In so doing Wright rejects the underlying assumptions and values of the neoclassical economic model discussed in the earlier

parts of this book (chapters 2 and 3)˙and consequently
rejects the alleged benefits of such a market model.
Wright's opinion asks the attorney to look at each
individual buyer and to make a personal, what I would
call a "status", determination about that individual. On
such a personal level, law is required to either confirm
or destroy the terms of a written contract. While the
outcome may seem "fair" or "equitable" it is undoubtedly an outcome far different than would be rendered
by a judge that accepted the operation of a competitive
marketplace, that accepted the "sanctity" of a written
contract, or that ultimately felt individuals had a duty,
on their own to protect themselves. That is, the first
line of defense for every consumer is to protect your-
self—be a smart consumer. Believing in the marketplace, believing in alternative choices rather than subju-
gation and exploitation could easily lead to a different
result in a case such as this. If one believes a reasonable opportunity for competition exists and that consumers have market power and choice, then a decision that
tells the consumer to be more careful would be in order,
absent the proof of market failure and lack of alternatives.

  According to the plan of this book—the reader
need not be for or against Wright's position in this case.
The important point is to see that certain underlying
views about economic, political, and sociological relationships will have an effect on the direction of law.
This point will be even more evident when we look at
the next case on landlord and tenant relationships which
is also an opinion by Judge Skelly Wright.

Suggested Reading

Books

J. Calamari & J. Perillo, CONTRACTS 397–434 (3rd. ed. 1987).

R. Posner, ECONOMIC ANALYSIS OF LAW 79–126 (1986).

J. White & R. Summers, UNIFORM COMMERCIAL CODE 181–211 (3rd. ed. 1988).

Articles

Dalzell, *Duress by Economic Pressure,* 20 N.C.L.REV. 237 (1942).

Epstein, *Unconscionability: A Critical Reappraisal,* 18 J.LAW & ECON. 293 (1975).

Goldberg, *Institutional Change and the Quasi—Invisible Hand,* 17 J.LAW & ECON. 461 (1974).

Kennedy, *Distributive and Paternalist Motives in Contract and Tort Law, With Special Reference to Compulsory Terms and Unequal Bargaining Power,* 41 MD.L.REV. 563 (1982).

Kornhauser, *Unconscionability in Standard Forms,* 64 CALIF.L.REV. 1151 (1976).

Trebilcock, *The Doctrine of Inequality of Bargaining Power: Post–Benthamite Economics in the House of Lords,* 26 U.TORONTO L.J. 359 (1976).

Chapter Ten

PROPERTY LAW: THE IMPLIED WARRANTY OF HABITABILITY

JAVINS v. FIRST NATIONAL REALTY CORP.
United States Court of Appeals, District of Columbia Circuit, 1970.
428 F.2d 1071.

J. SKELLY WRIGHT, CIRCUIT JUDGE: These cases present the question whether housing code violations which arise during the term of a lease have any effect upon the tenant's obligation to pay rent. The Landlord and Tenant Branch of the District of Columbia Court of General Sessions ruled proof of such violations inadmissible when proffered as a defense to an eviction action for nonpayment of rent. The District of Columbia Court of Appeals upheld this ruling.

We now reverse and hold that a warranty of habitability, measured by the standards set out in the Housing Regulations for the District of Columbia, is implied by operation of law into leases of urban dwelling units covered by those Regulations and that breach of this warranty gives rise to the usual remedies for breach of contract.

I

The facts revealed by the record are simple. By separate written leases, each of the appellants rented an apartment in a three-building apartment complex in

113

Northwest Washington known as Clifton Terrace. The landlord, First National Realty Corporation, filed separate actions * * * on April 8, 1966, seeking possession on the ground that each of the appellants had defaulted in the payment of rent due for the month of April. The tenants, appellants here, admitted that they had not paid the landlord any rent for April. However, they alleged numerous violations of the Housing Regulations as "an equitable defense or [a] claim by way of recoupment or set-off of an amount equal to the rent claim,"

Since, in traditional analysis, a lease was the conveyance of an interest in land, courts have usually utilized the special rules governing real property transactions to resolve controversies involving leases. However, as the Supreme Court has noted in another context, "the body of private property law * * *, more than almost any other branch of law, has been shaped by distinctions whose validity is largely historical." Courts have a duty to reappraise old doctrines in the light of the facts and values of contemporary life—particularly old common law doctrines which the courts themselves created and developed. As we have said before, "[T]he continued vitality of the common law * * * depends upon its ability to reflect contemporary community values and ethics."

The assumption of landlord-tenant law, derived from feudal property law, that a lease primarily conveyed to the tenant an interest in land may have been reasonable in a rural, agrarian society; it may continue to be reasonable in some leases involving farming or commercial land. In these cases, the value of the lease to the tenant is the land itself. But in the case of the modern apartment dweller, the value of the lease is that it gives him a place to live. The city dweller who seeks to lease an apartment on the third floor of a tenement has little interest in the land 30 or 40 feet below, or even in the bare right of possession within the four walls of his apartment. When American city dwellers, both rich and poor, seek "shelter" today, they seek a well known package of goods and services—a package which includes not merely walls and ceilings, but also adequate heat, light and ventilation, serviceable plumbing facilities, secure windows and doors, proper sanitation, and proper maintenance.

Some courts have realized that certain of the old rules of property law governing leases are inappropriate for today's transactions. In order to reach results more in accord with the legitimate expectations of the parties and the standards of the community, courts have been gradually introducing more modern precepts of contract law in interpreting leases.

In our judgment the trend toward treating leases as contracts is wise and well considered.

Modern contract law has recognized that the buyer of goods and services in an industrialized society must rely upon the skill and honesty of the supplier to assure that goods and services purchased are of adequate quality. In interpreting most contracts, courts have sought to protect the legitimate expectations of the buyer and have steadily widened the seller's responsibility for the quality of goods and services through implied warranties of fitness and merchantability.

The rigid doctrines of real property law have tended to inhibit the application of implied warranties to transactions involving real estate.

The common law rule absolving the lessor of all obligation to repair originated in the early Middle Ages. Such a rule was perhaps well suited to an agrarian economy; the land was more important than whatever small living structure was included in the leasehold, and the tenant farmer was fully capable of making repairs himself. These historical facts were the basis on which the common law constructed its rule; they also provided the necessary prerequisites for its application.

Today's urban tenants, the vast majority of whom live in multiple dwelling houses are interested, not in the land, but solely in "a house suitable for occupation." Furthermore, today's city dweller usually has a single, specialized skill unrelated to maintenance work; he is unable to make repairs like the "jack-of-all-trades" farmer who was the common law's model of the leassee. Further, unlike his agrarian predecessor who often remained on one piece of land for his entire life urban tenants today are more mobile than ever before. A tenant's tenure in a specific apartment will often not be sufficient to justify efforts at repairs. In addition, the increasing complexity of today's dwellings renders them much more difficult to repair than the structures of earlier times. In a multiple dwelling repair may require access to equipment and areas in the control of the landlord. Low and middle income tenants, even if they were interested in making repairs, would be unable to obtain any financing for major repairs and they have no long-term interest in the property.

Even beyond the rationale of traditional products liability law, the relationship of landlord and tenant suggests further compelling reasons for the law's protection of the tenants' legitimate expectations of quality. The inequality in bargaining power between landlord and tenant has been well documented. Tenants have very little leverage to enforce demands for better housing. Various impediments to competition in the rental housing market, such as racial and class discrimination and standardized form leases, mean that landlords place tenants in a take it or leave it situation. The increasingly severe shortage of adequate housing further increases the landlord's bargaining power and escalates the need for maintaining and improving the existing stock. Finally, the findings by various studies of the social impact of bad housing has led to the realization that poor housing is detrimental to the whole society, not merely to the unlucky ones who must suffer the daily indignity of living in a slum.

We therefore hold that the Housing Regulations imply a warranty of habitability, measured by the standards which they set out, into leases of all housing that they cover.

In *Javins* Judge Skelly Wright breaks new ground in the legal relationship between landlord and tenant by establishing an implied warranty of habitability for rental housing.   Judge Wright took an activist role in reforming the law in this area and his opinions in this area reflect the same type of philosophical disposition as was evident in his contract law cases such as *Williams v. Walker-Thomas Furniture Co.*[1] Considering his role in the dramatic change to landlord and tenant law, Judge Wright was asked to express his thoughts concerning the subject in a letter to Professor Edward Rabin.[2] In that letter Judge Wright expressed some of his personal thoughts on the subject.   His thoughts candidly illustrate the significant impact of his own use of law in his powerful role as a Judge on the D.C. Circuit Court of Appeals.

In key passages from the letter, Judge Wright responds to Professor Rabin's inquiry as follows:

---

1. *See* Chapter Nine.

2. Rabin, *The Revolution in Residential Landlord–Tenant Law: Causes and Consequences,* 69 CORNELL L.REV. 517, 549 (1984).

Why the revolution in landlord-tenant law is largely traceable to the 1960's rather than decades before I really cannot say with any degree of certainty.

* * * I was indeed influenced by the fact that, during the nationwide racial turmoil of the Sixties and the unrest caused by the injustice of racially Selective Service in Vietnam, most of the tenants in Washington, D.C. slums were poor and black and most of the landlords were rich and white. There is no doubt in my mind that these conditions played a subconscious role in influencing my landlord and tenant decisions.

* * * I didn't like what I saw, and I did what I could to ameliorate, if not eliminate, the injustice involved in the way many of the poor were required to live in the nation's capital.

I offer no apology for not following more closely the legal precedents which had cooperated in creating the conditions that I found unjust.[3]

These comments by Judge Wright reveal the nature and importance of one's subjective "World View" in the process of our legal evolution. Rightly or wrongly, Judge Wright felt that his judicial power extended to personally revising laws that he felt contributed to the continuation of an improper and exploitive relationship between landlords (rich Whites) and tenants (poor Blacks). Such a view not only demonstrates the way in which underlying philosophical views can affect law but it also illustrates how they can affect the Judge's conception of his role within the legal framework. Judge Wright clearly acknowledges a personal commitment to changing "bad" law in a way that enters current debates about, judicial activism. Keep in mind that the right-

---

3. *Id.*

ness or wrongness of Wright's views are not as fundamental to our study here, as is the understanding that
one's underlying views on key economic, political, and
social issues plays a significant role in giving direction to
their socially contextual understanding of law.

In many ways the *Javins* case reveals itself as
presenting many of the same economic issues, class and
race based issues, and underlying ideological issues as
did *Williams v. Walker–Thomas Furniture Co.*. A major
premise of the case is that no competitive market is at
work in the landlord tenant situation as viewed by
Judge Wright, or if there is such a market that the
market does not help tenant consumers in the way that
most economists would suggest. The case, however,
offers no evidence to support any conclusions regarding
lack of competition or lack of a market, rather the case
presumes that landlords exercise inordinate power over
the rental housing market and that tenants are exploited
by this power arrangement. The only evidence offered
to support this is that certain tenant housing is in bad
condition.

Judge Wright seeks to correct the apparent imbalance in power between landlords and tenants by requiring all landlords to keep their rental units in repair so
that they will be habitable throughout the entire term of
the lease. Economically, what does this decision mean?
Habitability is a relative concept but it requires upkeep
and imposes a cost on some landlords. This cost has
to be covered somehow. It can be covered by making
the landlord absorb the cost out of its profit margin, but
if profits are reduced below the market rate landlords
will abandon the rental housing market. Note, the
court makes no finding in *Javins* with respect to the
landlord's profit margin—was it excessive—when compared to landlords that rent to low-income tenants that
have a high risk of default and who historically provide

more wear and tear on apartments than say your middle class family with no children. If the market is shown to be competitive, then economic theory would hold that by definition these landlords were not earning any excessive rate of return. If this were the case there would be no excessive profit margin from which to cover the landlords' increased cost. The only other way to cover the costs of continued habitability would be through government subsidies.

The recent history of landlord and tenant relations continues from the groundwork set by Judge Wright in *Javins*. The emphasis has been to assume either a market failure or to more simply ignore market issues altogether because of a belief that markets don't really work—that is to say that market theories offered by most economists are merely elaborate systems of justification for the continuation of exploitation by those in power (landlords) against those without power (tenants). As a natural consequence of this underlying philosophical viewpoint much of America's recent housing policy has been designed to make landlords' absorb the cost of providing better and better accommodations to tenants. Some of the responses by landlords and developers might have been predictable by using basic economic theory.[4] For instance, landlords were required by court decision and by statutory acts to improve the habitability of rental units and to be more responsive to tenants. The landlord response was to offset the added cost by passing it on to the tenants by increasing rents. The legislative response was to get more involved in rent controls that restricted or prohibited the landlord from raising rents. Landlords then began to find that other real estate investments were more profitable so they

---

4. *See* Hoeflich & Malloy, *The Shattered Dream of American Housing Policy—The Need for Reform*, 26 B.C.L.Rev. 655 (1985).

started converting rental units to home ownership units in the form of condominiums and cooperatives. The legislative response to this move was to restrict and prevent the ability of a landlord to convert rental property to ownership form. The predictable result was for landlords to simply try to abandon some projects altogether. But even this lead to the strange result in one California case where a landlord was not allowed to close his apartment building, not allowed to convert it, not allowed to raise rent, and required to make improvements that would not be covered by the rent controls set for his building—in other words the law required him to continue operating his business at a loss for a use he did not wish to make.[5]

This entire history of landlord and tenant regulation has arguably also had an effect on discouraging new entrants into the rental housing market and has thus added to the shortage of rental vacancies in many large urban areas. Some would even argue that this has also added to the problem of homelessness.[6]

Certainly the way in which you view the history of landlord and tenant relations is dependent upon your underlying ideological perspective. The above rendition of events between landlord and legislative responses can be viewed as entirely predictable in a competitive economic model. In this context proponents of the free market can interpret these events as evidence that the legislation has been misguided in its efforts to correct the problems of a shortage of decent and affordable rental housing. On the other hand, if you don't believe in the assumptions, norms, and values of the market

---

5. *See* Guerther, *Landlord's Unusual Response to Rent Control Stirs Fight,* WALL ST.J., Mar. 21, 1984, at 31.

6. Urban Land Institute, *New York Study Links Homelessness to Rent Control,* 21 LAND USE DIG. 1 (Aug. 1989).

model, or if you don't believe there is any competition in the rental housing market, then you might interpret these "facts" differently. The same chain of events could be interpreted as evidence of the market power and exploitiveness of landlords; that at every turn they seek to circumvent and undercut the legislative and judicial efforts to help disempowered consumer/tenants. Indeed, the history shows the need for even more government involvement in order to correct the imbalance of power between landlords and tenants.

Thus, one's underlying view of economic relationships affects one's view of law and legal recourse. Judge Skelly Wright, as a judicial reformer, represents a view of the law that is more sympathetic to the economic approaches of liberal and left communitarian legal economists then to the approach of conservatives or libertarians. He is, likewise, more interested in context specific facts and *standards* than in *legal rules*. Classical liberals would be somewhere in the middle. On the one hand, the classical liberal approach would consider the potential for abuse and exploitation of tenants in the marketplace and would be sensitive to the need to provide every human being with a decent shelter. On the other hand, classical liberals would likely be much more sensitive to the marketplace. That is to say, landlords' would not be fully to blame for acting as economically rational actors. If, as a society, we are committed to providing adequate shelter for everyone, then as a society we should pay for it and not try and extract social costs from one group of individuals; landlords. Furthermore, the classical liberal response would acknowledge the correctness of economic theory in telling us that rent controls and anti-conversion legislation are ineffective ways to resolve our rental housing problems. Classical liberals would seek to simulate market responses to correct these social problems and that might include such things as using general tax revenues to provide housing vouchers to needy individuals that could then procure rental housing in an otherwise "normal" rental housing market.

Again, as in the case of contract unconscionability the law, and one's understanding of the underlying facts, can be influenced by the philosophical and ideological perspective that is brought to the resolution of these difficult and pressing social problems.

Suggested Reading

Books

R. Cunningham, W. Stoebuck, & D. Whitman, THE LAW
OF PROPERTY 255–409 (1984).

RESOLVING THE HOUSING CRISIS: GOVERNMENT POLICY,
DECONTROL, AND THE PUBLIC INTEREST (M. Johnson
ed. 1982).

Articles

Ackerman, *More on Slum Housing and Redistribution
Policy: A Reply to Professor Komesar,* 82 YALE
L.J. 1194 (1973).

Ackerman, *Regulating Slum Housing Markets on Behalf
of the Poor: Of Housing Codes, Housing Subsidies
and Income Redistribution Policy,* 80 YALE L.J.
1093 (1971).

Brackel & McIntyre, *The Uniform Residential Landlord
and Tenant Act (URLTA) in Operation: Two Re-
ports,* 1980 AM.B.FOUND. 555.

Hirsch, Hirsch & Margolis, *Regression Analysis of the
Effects of Habitability Laws Upon Rent: An Empirical Observation of the Ackerman–Komesar Debate,*
63 CALIF.L.REV. 1098 (1975).

Hoeflich & Malloy, *The Shattered Dream of American
Housing Policy—The Need for Reform,* 26 B.C.L.
REV. 655 (1985).

Kennedy, *The Effect of the Warranty of Habitability On
Low Income Housing: "Milking" And Class Vio-
lence,* 15 FLA.ST.U.L.REV. 485 (1987).

Komesar, *Return to Slumsville: A Critique of The Ackerman Analysis of Housing Code Enforcement and
the Poor,* 82 YALE L.J. 1175 (1973).

Meyers, *The Covenant of Habitability and the American
Law Institute,* 27 STAN.L.REV. 879 (1975).

Rabin, *The Revolution in Residential Landlord–Tenant Law: Causes and Consequences,* 69 CORNELL L.REV. 517 (1984).

Chapter Eleven

CRIMINAL/
CONSTITUTIONAL LAW:
RIGHT TO COUNSEL

MERRITT v. FAULKNER
United States Court of Appeals, Seventh Circuit, 1983.
697 F.2d 761.

SWYGERT, SENIOR CIRCUIT JUDGE.

This appeal primarily concerns the right to appointed counsel and the right to a jury trial of an indigent prisoner who seeks relief for the alleged deliberate indifference of prison officials to his serious medical problems. This district court denied the prisoner's request for appointed counsel, as well as his motions for a jury trial, appointment of an independent medical expert, and enforcement of a subpoena. After trial, the district court found for the defendants. We find that the denials of the motions for appointed counsel and for a jury trial were abuses of discretion.

On July 10, 1978, Billy Merritt, a prisoner at the Indiana State Prison, injured his left eye. He complained of blurred vision and was seen, two days later, by Dr. Saylors, a physician on the prison staff. Saylors could not determine whether there was any damage to the eye, but he felt the complaint was serious enough to act on it promptly. He referred Merritt to the prison consultant ophthalmologist, Dr. Houck. Saylors indicated in Merritt's file that the matter was "urgent."

Houck, examining Merritt the next day, found that Merritt had a vitreous hemorrhage in the left eye. About a month after the accident, Houck arranged for Merritt to be tested for sickle cell disease. The test was positive. Houck thought there might be a relationship between the sickle cell disease and the hemorrhaging in the left eye, but he did not know anything about the treatment of sickle cell disease. Houck examined Merritt three times during the next three months, but he did not prescribe any treatment or make any referrals. Saylors described Houck's handling Merritt's medical condition as "unusual." Five months after the injury, in December 1978, Houck referred Merritt to a consulting surgeon for consideration of a vitrectomy, an operation which could remove fluid from Merritt's left eye.

During this period Merritt, however, was examined by another prison staff physician. This physician noted that Merritt's left eye was still hemorrhaging. Although this doctor referred Merritt to the prison's assistant administrator of medical services for treatment, including surgery, no other operation was performed.

Indigent civil litigants have no constitutional or statutory right to be represented by a lawyer. Nevertheless, particularly when rights of a constitutional dimension are at stake, a poor person's access to the federal courts must not be turned into an exercise in futility.

In some civil cases meaningful access requires representation by a lawyer.

Even when there is no absolute right to counsel * * * the Court has made it clear that the circumstances of a particular case may make the presence of counsel necessary.

One important reason for representation by counsel is ensuring the efficacy and accuracy of the factfinding process. Quite often the factual and legal issues in a civil case are more complex than in a criminal case.

It is within this context that this Circuit has fashioned standards for the exercise of discretion in considering whether to appoint counsel for indigent civil litigants in the federal courts under 28 U.S.C. Sec. 1915(d) (1976). In *Maclin v. Freake,* 650 F.2d 885 (1981) (per curiam), we set forth and applied five nonexclusive factors which a district court should consider in ruling upon such a request. See also *McKeever v. Israel,* 689 F.2d 1315 (7th Cir.1982). These factors are: (1) whether the merits of the indigent's claim are colorable; (2) the ability of the indigent plaintiff to investigate crucial facts; (3) whether the nature of the evidence indicates that the truth will more likely be exposed where both sides are represented by counsel; (4) the capability of the indigent litigant to present the case; and (5) the complexity of the legal issues raised by the complaint.

Analysis of these five factors indicates that the district court abused its discretion when it denied Merritt's request for appointed counsel.

The judgment of the district court is hereby reversed. This cause is remanded for a new trial in which a jury and appointed counsel are provided to the plaintiff-appellant.

POSNER, CIRCUIT JUDGE, concurring in part and dissenting in part.

I disagree, however, that it was an abuse of discretion for the district court not to appoint counsel for Merritt. For reasons explained in my dissenting opinion in *McKeever v. Israel,* 689 F.2d 1315, 1324-25 (7th Cir. 1982), I believe the presumption should be against appointment of counsel in prisoner civil rights cases. One of the reasons given in my dissent in *McKeever* is especially applicable to this case. I said that a prisoner who has a good damages suit should be able to hire a competent lawyer and that by making the prisoner go this route we subject the probable merit of his case to the test of the market. Merritt alleges that the defendants are legally responsible for his blindness. If this were so, we would have a case that was attractive to many personal-injury lawyers, even apart from the fillip of an award of attorney's fees if the plaintiff prevails.

But all other differences between the civil and criminal settings to one side, a plaintiff in a damages case has better access than a criminal defendant to the private market in lawyers. The criminal defendant does not get a sum of money out of which he can pay his lawyer if he wins. But a prisoner who can prove he was wrongfully blinded can look forward to a very big money judgment to share with his lawyer and to an award of attorney's fees under section 1988 besides. I do not think we need worry that a prisoner who has a good case will have difficulty getting the name of a lawyer. If Merritt had a good case this or another lawyer would have been happy to handle it on a contingent-fee basis, with the prospect of an award of attorney's fees under 42 U.S.C. Sec. 1988 as an additional inducement.

The court states: "An underlying assumption of the adversarial system is that both parties will have roughly equal legal resources." This has never been an assumption of the adversarial system. We do not put a cap on the amount of money that a litigant can spend on lawyers; we do not inquire whether the litigants had roughly equal legal resources; we allow one to outspend the other by as much as he pleases. We count on the courts not to be overawed by the litigant with the higher-priced counsel. But, whether it is right or wrong, the goal of equalizing legal resources implies, I admit, that every indigent civil litigant should have, at the very least, counsel appointed for him; and I worry that this proposition may be the unstated premise of the majority opinion—the stated but unsupported premise of which is that Merritt had a good case yet, mysteriously, could not find a lawyer to represent him.

Merritt v. Faulkner is an interesting case because of the contrasting mindframe as between the majority opinion expressed by Judge Swygert and the dissenting opinion of Judge Posner. The case involves the right to counsel for an indigent prisoner. The majority opinion takes a decidedly non-market approach to this issue and tries to establish the appropriate grounds upon which a prisoner should be entitled to a state appointed counsel. In the majority opinion five criteria are set out and they focus on the merits of the indigents' claim, the ability of the indigent to investigate crucial facts, the likelihood that evidence can be produced effectively without counsel, the ability of the indigent to present their own case, and the complexity of the legal issues involved. Much like the opinions of Judge Skelly Wright, the majority in *Merritt* seeks a personal and context oriented approach to discussing access to legal empowerment.

In contrast to the majority, Judge Posner's dissent provides an analysis of the indigent's claim to legal counsel based on a conservative market model. Consistent with the discussion of Judge Posner in Chapter Four, the belief in neoclassical economic theory presents a different approach to the same set of facts. Judge Posner apparently believes that there should be a presumption against appointment of counsel in a prisoner civil rights case. A major reason for this belief is centered upon basic conservative notions of a competitive marketplace. Posner asserts that a prisoner with a strong case, a strong chance of winning in a claim against the state, would be able to get a private attorney without having one appointed and without having to expend his own resources to hire the attorney. In our adversarial system an attorney could take such a case on a contingency-fee basis and thus redress the wrong committed while providing a recovery for the injured indigent and doing so at no out of pocket cost to the client.

Posner's formulation of the market for legal services assumes that prisoners have access to outside lawyers that will compete and evaluate the merits of a claim. By definition his opinion also assumes that this is a normatively good way to "objectively" determine the merits of an indigent's claim. If the market does not provide an attorney then the client is probably without a meritorious claim and, therefore, without a need for the services requested. This line of analysis is consistent with general market theory whereby the economist would assert that if a product is not produced in a competitive market or if certain contract terms are used in a competitive market than these must, by definition, be the terms that customers want, that is the terms or products that customers are willing to pay for. In the context of conservative marketplace analysis, the end objective is to find or create a good functioning marketplace and then results that flow from that market model can be upheld as objective displays of individual choice rather than personal renditions of what judges feel a customer or a client *should* want or *should* be supplied by society.

One should ask if the indigent prisoner, forced to contend with the prison system and the many sources of official and non-official power over their daily activities, is any more empowered than the poor tenants or consumers in the two Skelly Wright opinions discussed in the preceding chapters. Is Posner speaking for "everyone" when he says that it has never been an assumption of our adversarial system that both parties will have roughly equal legal resources? And further consider how such a view is consistent with conservative market theory in general. It is consistent in that the market model operates on the understanding of a non-equal distribution of wealth and resources. An inherent assumption of the market model, as discussed in Chapter Three, is that this unequal distribution is not assumed to be unfair and furthermore the outcomes generated by the market model, which is driven by the command power of those with the greater allocation of resources, is understood to be fair. From this ideological vantage point it is easy to see how someone like Judge Posner could be comfortable with legal outcomes even in the face of tremendous disparities in legal services available to each side of an adversarial dispute. Furthermore, it is possible to understand why there is a feeling of fairness and justice in not compelling the state to provide legal counsel to an indigent prisoner with a civil claim. Judges like Posner are not necessarily cruel and heartless enemies of the indigent but rather they see and define justice from a different ideological perspective than do judges from different ideological schools of thought.

Suggested Readings

Books

W. LaFave & J. Israel, CRIMINAL PROCEDURE 260–319 (1985).

W. LaFave & J. Israel, 2 CRIMINAL PROCEDURE–CRIMINAL PRACTICE SERIES 11 (1984).

R. McKenzie & G. Tullock, THE NEW WORLD OF ECONOMICS: EXPLORATIONS INTO THE HUMAN EXPERIENCE 129–156 (1975).

L. Phillips & H. Votey, ECONOMIC ANALYSIS OF PRESSING SOCIAL PROBLEMS 309–338 (1974).

R. Posner, ECONOMIC ANALYSIS OF LAW 201–228, 517–553 (1986).

Articles

Clermont & Currivan, *Improving on the Contingent Fee,* 63 CORNELL L.REV. 529 (1978).

Posner, *An Economic Theory of the Criminal Law,* 85 COLUM.L.REV. 1193 (1985).

Schwartz and Mitchell, *An Economic Analysis of the Contingent Fee in Personal Injury Litigation,* 22 STAN.L.REV. 1125 (1970).

Chapter Twelve

EMPLOYMENT LAW: COMPARABLE WORTH

AMERICAN NURSES' ASSOC. v. ILLINOIS
United States Court of Appeals, Seventh Circuit, 1986.
783 F.2d 716.

POSNER, Circuit Judge.

This class action charges the State of Illinois with sex discrimination in employment, in violation of Title VII of the Civil Rights Act of 1964, 42 U.S.C. Sec. 2000e, and the equal protection clause of the Fourteenth Amendment. The named plaintiffs are two associations of nurses plus 21 individuals, mostly but not entirely female, who work for the state in jobs such as nursing and typing that are filled primarily by women. The suit is on behalf of all state employees in these job classifications. The precise allegations of the complaint will require our careful attention later, but for now it is enough to note that they include as an essential element the charge that the state pays workers in predominantly male job classifications a higher wage not justified by any difference in the relative worth of the predominantly male and the predominantly female jobs in the state's roster.

In April 1985 the district judge dismissed the complaint under Fed.R.Civ.P. 12(b)(6) but without ruling on the state's alternative request for summary judgment, 606 F.Supp. 1313. The ground for dismissal was that the complaint pleaded a comparable worth case and that a failure to pay employees in accordance with comparable worth does not violate federal antidiscrimination law. The plaintiffs appeal.

Comparable worth is not a legal concept, but a shorthand expression for the movement to raise the ratio of wages in traditionally women's jobs to wages in traditionally men's jobs. Its premises are both historical and cognitive. The historical premise is that a society politically and culturally dominated by men steered women into certain jobs and kept the wages in those jobs below what the jobs were worth, precisely because most of the holders were women. The cognitive premise is that analytical techniques exist for determining the relative worth of jobs that involve different levels of skill, effort, risk, responsibility, etc. These premises are vigorously disputed on both theoretical and empirical grounds. Economists point out that unless employers forbid women to compete for the higher-paying, traditionally men's jobs—which would violate federal law—women will switch into those jobs until the only difference in wage between traditionally women's jobs and traditionally men's jobs will be that necessary to equate the supply of workers in each type of job to the demand. Economists have conducted studies which show that virtually the entire difference in the average hourly wage of men and women, including that due to the fact that men and women tend to be concentrated in different types of job, can be explained by the fact that most women take considerable time out of the labor force in order to take care of their children. As a result they tend to invest less in their "human capital" (earning capacity); and since part of any wage is a return on human capital, they tend therefore to be found in jobs that pay less. Consistently with this hypothesis, the studies find that women who have never married earned as much as men who have never married. To all this the advocates of comparable worth reply that although there are no longer explicit barriers to women's entering traditionally men's jobs, cultural and psychological barriers remain as a result of which many though not all women internalize men's expectations regarding jobs appropriate for women and therefore invest less in their human capital.

On the cognitive question economists point out that the ratio of wages in different jobs is determined by the market rather than by an a priori conception of relative merit, in just the same way that the ratio of the price of caviar to the price of cabbage is determined by relative scarcity rather than relative importance to human welfare. Upsetting the market equilibrium by imposing such a conception would have costly consequences, some of which might undercut the ultimate goals of the comparable worth movement. If the movement should cause wages in traditionally men's jobs to be depressed below their market level and wages in traditionally women's jobs to be jacked above their market level, women will have less incentive to enter traditionally men's fields and more to enter traditionally women's fields. Analysis cannot stop there, because the change in relative wages will send men in the same direction: fewer men will enter the traditionally men's jobs, more the traditionally women's jobs. As a result there will be more room for women in traditionally men's jobs and at the same time fewer opportunities for women in traditionally women's jobs—especially since the number of those jobs will shrink as employers are induced by the higher wage to substitute capital for labor inputs (e.g., more word processors, fewer secretaries). Labor will be allocated less efficiently; men and women alike may be made worse off.

Against this the advocates of comparable worth urge that collective bargaining, public regulation of wages and hours, and the lack of information and mobility of some workers make the market model an inaccurate description of how relative wages are determined and how they influence the choice of jobs. The point has particular force when applied to a public employer such as the State of Illinois, which does not have the same incentives that a private firm would have to use labor efficiently. An employer (private or public) that simply pays the going wage in each of the different types of job in its establishment, and makes no effort to discourage women from applying for particular jobs or to steer them toward particular jobs, would be justifiably surprised to discover that it may be violating federal law because each wage rate and therefore the ratio between them have been found to be determined by cultural or psychological factors attributable to the history of male domination of society: that it has to hire a consultant to find out how it must, regardless of market conditions, change the wages it pays, in order to achieve equity between traditionally male and traditionally female jobs; and that it must pay backpay, to boot.

The circuits that have considered this contention have rejected it.

All that this seems to mean * * * is "that even absent a showing of equal work, there is a cause of action under Title VII when there is direct evidence that an employer has *intentionally* depressed a woman's salary because she is a woman. The decision today does not approve a cause of action based on a *comparison* of the wage rates of dissimilar jobs." The relevance of a comparable worth study in proving sex discrimination is that it may provide the occasion on which the employer is forced to declare his intentions toward his female employees.

The plaintiffs can get no mileage out of casting a comparable worth case as an equal protection case. The Supreme Court held in *Washington v. Davis,* 426

U.S. 229, 96 S.Ct. 2040, 48 L.Ed.2d 597 (1976), that the equal protection clause is violated only by intentional discrimination; the fact that a law or official practice adopted for a lawful purpose has a racially differential impact is not enough. The Court applied this principle to sex discrimination in *Personnel Administrator of Massachusetts v. Feeney*, 442 U.S. 256, 99 S.Ct. 2282, 60 L.Ed.2d 870 (1979).

But when intentional discrimination is charged under Title VII the inquiry is the same as in an equal protection case. The difference between the statutory and constitutional prohibitions becomes important only when a practice is challenged not because it is intended to hurt women (say) but because it hurts them inadvertently and is not justified by the employer's needs—when, in short, the challenge is based on a theory of "disparate impact," as distinct from "disparate treatment" (intentional discrimination). The plaintiffs in this case, however, have said that they are proceeding on the basis of disparate treatment rather than disparate impact.

So if all that the plaintiffs in this case are complaining about is the State of Illinois' failure to implement a comparable worth study, they have no case and it was properly dismissed. We must therefore consider what precisely they are complaining about.

Maybe the allegations in paragraph 9 are illuminated by subsequent paragraphs of the complaint. Paragraph 10, after summarizing the comparable worth study says, "Defendants knew or should have known of the historical and continuing existence of patterns and practices of discrimination in compensation and classification. For example, an electrician whose job is rated in the study at only 274 points in skill, responsibility, etc. has an average monthly salary of $2,826, compared to $2,104 for a nurse whose job is rated at 480 points. These disparities are consistent, however, with the state's paying market wages, and of course the fact that the state knew that market wages do not always comport with the principles of comparable worth would not make a refusal to abandon the market actionable under Title VII.

After reading the comparable worth study the responsible state officials knew that the state's compensation system might not be consistent with the principles of comparable worth ("might" because there has been no determination that the comparable worth study is valid even on its own terms—maybe it's a lousy comparable worth study). But it would not follow that their failure to implement the study was willful in a sense relevant to liability under Title VII. They may have decided not to implement it because implementation would cost too much or lead to excess demand for some jobs and insufficient demand for others. The only thing that would make the failure a form of intentional and therefore actionable sex discrimination would be if the motivation for not implementing the study was the sex of the employees—if for example the officials thought that men ought to be paid more than women even if there is no difference in skill or effort or in the conditions of work.

Before concluding that the district court should not have dismissed the complaint we must consider whether anything happened between the filing of the complaint and the district court's decision to show that the plaintiffs really were pleading just a comparable worth case.

It is premature to conclude that there is no worthwhile remedy for the intentional discrimination that consists of overpaying workers in predominantly male jobs because most of those workers are male. We emphasize, however, that proof of this causality is essential and is not to be inferred merely from the results of a comparable worth study and from the refusal of the employer to implement the study's recommendations. We do not want to arouse false hopes; the plaintiffs have a tough row to hoe. They may lose eventually on summary judgment if discovery yields no more evidence than is contained in the unsupported assertions and stale and seemingly isolated incidents in the plaintiffs' exhibits. But the plaintiffs are entitled to make additional efforts to prove a case of intentional discrimination within the boundaries sketched in this opinion.

Reversed and Remanded.

American Nurses raises the question of comparable worth as the basis for salary determinations between various job types and categories. While the legal right to demand comparable worth has not yet been fully recognized, this case and decision by Judge Posner help to illustrate the emerging lines of argument that are being used in this "cutting edge" social policy debate. The comparable worth issue is one that tries to address perceived disparities in the incomes of women and men. At one level there are complaints that men and women doing the same jobs earn different income—for example women attorneys earn less on average than do male attorneys. Justifications for such discrepancies usually relate to the number of years the average woman and man have been in the work force, the continuity of the work force participation, the hours worked, the type and size of firm worked for, etc. In accounting for all of these demographic differences many economists explain away much of the alleged disparity in pay for the "same" work. The second level of analysis goes beyond a comparison of income within the same job type and looks instead at comparisons between different types of work. This second level of analysis is much more difficult to deal with and it is the primary focal point for the debates on comparable worth.

The comparable worth debate concerns the discrepancy of pay between different job types or categories. For example the Posner opinion cites evidence that the electrician makes more than a nurse. The question that comparable worth supporters are asking is why does the electrician make more than the nurse. Proponents of comparable worth want to conclude that electricians make more than nurses because electricians tend to be males and nurses tend to be women. Thus, the reason for the disparity in pay is due to an improper goal of a male dominated society to pay male job holders more money. By paying males more money males preserve a system of economic dominance over women. Comparable worth advocates argue that years of socialization and job steering have kept women in predominantly lower paying jobs despite the reduction or elimination of many absolute barriers to female participation in all aspects of the workforce and the economy. Because of this belief advocates of comparable worth seek to have job skills and responsibilities compared on a point schedule of difficulty and thereby make a more fair distribution of wealth to women by recognizing the complexity and difficulty of the work they are already performing. In other words, the position in favor of comparable worth is one that says women are currently being underpaid for the work that they perform and consequently the criteria used to legitimize the current pay distributions is unjust. It is in recognizing this underlying position of comparable worth advocates that one begins to appreciate the ideological distinctions that will come into play in public debate, legislation, and judicial adjudication on these issues.

The opinion of Judge Posner in *American Nurses* generally reflects the views of many market oriented philosophers concerning the matter of comparable worth. For market oriented thinkers distinctions in salary paid for various types of work are understood in the context of supply and demand. Likewise, disparities are justified and legitimized as the natural results of a well functioning marketplace. While barriers to job entry would violate the market approach, the elimination of unjustifiable bars to women taking certain types of jobs allows the market to reach fair and justifiable results, even when those results include paying predominantly female oriented jobs (nurse or secretary) less than predominantly male oriented jobs (electrician or construction worker).

From the vantage point of free market economics salaries and wages are determined by finding the market equilibrium between our supply and demand curves as discussed in Chapter Two. If a job requires less of an investment in human capital, is less dangerous to one's health, has more flexible work hours, or allows one more ability to interrupt the continuity of a career path, such as taking years off for child rearing, without unduly diminishing one's ability to reenter the marketplace, than such jobs will likely be able to pay a lesser salary to attract a sufficient supply than jobs with the opposite characteristics. Furthermore, if females find such lower paying jobs to be compatible with their interests or life style choices then they are merely getting what they desire—a wage they are willing to accept for a job they are willing to take. With this understanding of the marketplace there is no hidden conspiracy and no male oriented agenda to contend with.

The market theory uses the same method of analysis to explain differences in pay as between traditional male and female jobs as it does to explain instances of trash collectors in some cities earning more than school teachers or college educated government administrators. Likewise, the market model explains why law professors are paid more than history professors; because there are more alternatives or opportunity costs for the lawyer than for the historian. By comparable worth standards the history professor probably has spent more time getting a Ph.D. than the law professor getting a J.D., probably has a greater writing requirement for promotion and tenure, and probably has to spend substantially more time in the classroom teaching students. Is the law professor unfairly overpaid? Does the difference have anything to do with sex or race? The message here is of course that the answer to these questions has something to do with one's ideological viewpoint. The results of these pay differences are fair for the free market economists, in the sense that they are the cumulative results of innumerable individual choices by both buyers and sellers of labor. To force a different distribution of income on this arrangement would be to second guess and impose someone else's or some group's personal view as to a fair wage onto the private arrangements of millions of people. To allow comparable worth, in other words, is to suppose that some specially informed person or group can determine what people need or should get better than the individuals can determine themselves. Such an approach to market relationships would be the antithesis to free choice and liberty.

The view from the pro comparable worth perspective is quite different. The supporters of comparable worth have an underlying distrust or lack of faith in the marketplace theory of wage determination. For them it seems that market theory is offered as a justification or apology for a real world instance of exploitation and subordination of women to men. Both approaches—

comparable worth and market theory—speak in terms
of paying people what they are *worth* but the ideological distinctions focus on how to measure one's worth.
Instead of accepting outcomes generated by a biased
neoclassical model of the job market, comparable worth
supporters want to measure worth in terms of a different set of "objective" criteria. Instead of the "objective"
outcomes of a subjective market model—See Chapter
Two—comparable worth advocates seek to establish
objective point systems for classifying jobs. Unfortu-
nately, this system like the neoclassical economics they
reject, is inherently subjective—but at least it is a subjec-
tivity that is favorable to their economic and political
position. From this perspective they can view past and
current law as illegitimate and inherently unjust because
it is used to prop up an income distribution system that
is inherently unfair and which is the product of the
institutional exploitation and subordination of women.
Only by rejecting the market framework for social dialogue can comparable worth supporters shift the legal
structure to one that recognizes their claims.

The *American Nurses* case is a useful opinion for
this book because it illustrates how Judges like Posner
are unable to recognize, accept or properly contend with
the comparable worth dialogue because it fundamentally deals with a completely different set of ideological
norms and definitional understandings of such basic
terms as worth, value, justice, and fairness. The lesson
of this case and of this book is that the subjective
ideological views that we each carry are fundamental to
our understanding of the world around us. It means
further that our understanding and practice of law is
related to, and to a great extent derived from, our
underlying beliefs concerning the basis of economic and
political relationships in our society. Regardless of
what we believe, we will be ineffective as lawyers if we

cannot learn to understand and tune into these ideological differences. We must be able to understand the legal dialogue around us before we can hope to enter into and engage in any meaningful efforts to formulate change or to advance the interests of a client.

Suggested Readings

Books

P. Cox, EMPLOYMENT DISCRIMINATION Chap. 16 (1987).

C. McKinnon, TOWARD A FEMINIST THEORY OF THE STATE (1989).

E. Paul, EQUITY AND GENDER: THE COMPARABLE WORTH DEBATE (1989).

M. Player, EMPLOYMENT DISCRIMINATION LAW (1988).

D. Rhode, JUSTICE AND GENDER (1989).

T. Sowell, CIVIL RIGHTS: RHETORIC OR REALITY? (1984).

Articles

Becker, *Barriers Facing Women in the Wage Labor Market and the Need for Additional Remedies: A Reply to Fischel and Lazear,* 53 U.CHI.L.REV. 934 (1986).

Brown, Baumann & Melnick, *Equal Pay for Jobs of Comparable Worth: An Analysis of the Rhetoric,* 21 HARV.C.R.C.L.L.REV. 127 (1986).

Colker, *Anti–Subordination Above All: Sex, Race, and Equal Protection,* 61 N.Y.U.L.REV. 1003 (1986).

Donohue, *Further Thoughts on Employment Discrimination Legislation: A Reply to Judge Posner,* 136 U.PA.L.REV. 523 (1987).

Fischel & Lazear, *Comparable Worth: A Rejoinder,* 53 U.CHI.L.REV. 950 (1986).

Fischel & Lazear, *Comparable Worth and Discrimination in Labor Markets,* 53 U.CHI.L.REV. 891 (1986).

Holzhauer, *The Economic Possibilities of Comparable Worth,* 53 U.CHI.L.REV. 919 (1986).

Loudon & Loudon, *Applying Disparate Impact to Title VII Comparable Worth Claims: An Incomparable Task,* 61 IND.L.J. 165 (1986).

Newman & Vonhof, *Separate But Equal—Job Segregation and Pay Equity in the Wake of Gunther,* 1981 U.ILL.L.REV. 269.

Posner, *The Efficiency and the Efficacy of Title VII,* 136 U.PA.L.REV. 513 (1987).

Chapter Thirteen

TORT LAW: DESIGN SAFETY AND SOCIAL RESPONSIBILITY

GRIMSHAW v. FORD MOTOR CO.

Court of Appeal, Fourth District, Division 2, 1981.
119 Cal.App.3d 757, 174 Cal.Rptr. 348.

TAMURA, ACTING P.J.—A 1972 Ford Pinto hatchback automobile unexpectedly stalled on a freeway erupting into flames when it was rear ended by a car proceeding in the same direction. Mrs. Lilly Gray, the driver of the Pinto, suffered fatal burns and 13–year–old Richard Grimshaw, a passenger in the Pinto, suffered severe and permanently disfiguring burns on his face and entire body. Grimshaw and the heirs of Mrs. Gray (Grays) sued Ford Motor Company and others. Following a six-month jury trial, verdicts were returned in favor of plaintiffs against Ford Motor Company. Grimshaw was awarded $2,516,000 compensatory damages and $125 million punitive damages; the Grays were awarded $559,680 in compensatory damages. On Ford's motion for a new trial, Grimshaw was required to remit all but $3½ million of the punitive award as a condition of denial of the motion.

Ford appeals from the judgment and from an order denying its motion for a judgment notwithstanding the verdict as to punitive damages.

In 1968, Ford began designing a new subcompact automobile which ultimately became the Pinto. Mr. Iacocca, then a Ford vice president conceived the project and was its moving force. Ford's objective was to build a car at or below 2,000 pounds to sell for no more than $2,000.

When a prototype failed the fuel system integrity test, the standard of care for engineers in the industry was to redesign and retest it. The vulnerability of the production Pinto's fuel tank at speeds of 20 and 30 miles-per-hour fixed barrier tests could have been remedied by inexpensive "fixes", but Ford produced and sold the Pinto to the public without doing anything to remedy the defects.

Harley Copp, a former Ford engineer and executive in charge of the crash testing program, testified that the highest level of Ford's management made the decision to go forward with the production of the Pinto, knowing that the gas tank was vulnerable to puncture and rupture at low rear impact speeds creating a significant risk of death or injury from fire and knowing that "fixes" were feasible at nominal cost. He testified that management's decision was based on the cost savings which would inure from omitting or delaying the "fixes."

Finally, Mr. Copp testified to conversations in late 1968 or early 1969 with the chief assistant research engineer in charge of cost-weight evaluation of the Pinto, and to a later conversation with the chief chassis engineer who was then in charge of crash testing the early prototype. In these conversations, both men expressed concern about the integrity of the Pinto's fuel system and complained about management's unwillingness to deviate from the design if the change would cost money.

Grimshaw (by his guardian ad litem) and the Grays sued Ford and others.

Ford seeks reversal of the judgment as a whole.

In the ensuing analysis (ad nauseam) of Ford's wide-ranging assault on the judgment, we have concluded that Ford has failed to demonstrate that any errors or irregularities occurred during the trial which resulted in a miscarriage of justice requiring reversal.

The judgment in *Gray v. Ford Motor Co.* is affirmed.

———

The *Grimshaw* case makes a fitting example for our study of economic ideology and is well suited to be the last case in this series of examples. This case was chosen in part because it provides a familiar fact situation to a problem of tort law and thus helps to round out the basic topic areas for the book's illustrative cases. More importantly, the case provides a good illustration of the ideological assumptions of one of the parties to the suit. The *Grimshaw* case shows quite dramatically how the Ford Motor Co. used a "scientific" (cost and benefit) approach to social responsibility when it introduced a poorly designed vehicle to the public.

The Ford Motor Company, as evidenced by its own internal company memoranda, was aware of the design and explosion problems of the Pinto. By its own account, internal Ford documentation reveals that the company undertook to establish the expected payout rate or cost to them for potential death and injury claims of customers that might be injured by the explosive nature of the Pinto's design. This cost was compared to the cost of making design changes to the fuel tank of the automobile. The Ford cost and benefit analysis indicated that the cost of paying for an expected 180 burn deaths and 180 serious burn injuries per year would not make it cost-efficient to add an $11 part per car in order to prevent the harm.[1]

In terms of reducing these personal losses to dollar calculations, Ford assumed that it would cost $137 million to correct the problem with the Pinto's design and that the expected payout for death and injury claims would be about $49.5 million.[2] Simple economics told Ford that it made no sense to spend $137 million in order to save $49.5 million.

The approach of Ford to this problem can be understood in the context of our discussion of neoclassical economics. Ford was trying to make a decision on how to best use scarce resources. Traditional economic analysis revealed that the cost to change the design of the Pinto fuel system far exceeded the benefits by almost three to one. From a purely personal view this means that Ford would be better off, spend less of its resources, by paying death and injury claims than in changing the Pinto fuel system. Such a move would provide more profit to the company. Importantly, the Ford position must be thought of in a larger ideological context. The conservative and libertarian approaches to free market economics tell us that actors should not only act in their own personal interest but that in so acting they further the general social good at the same time. In other words, Ford's only moral duty is to maximize its corporate profit, to make efficient decisions. This self directed approach leads to the best use of scarce social resources and ultimately to the best social outcomes. Looked at in the best ideological light, therefore, Ford executives were not just profit seekers with no concern for the public, to the contrary,

1. See L., Strobel, RECKLESS HOMICIDE? 79–92, 286 (1980).

2. Id.

they could have legitimately thought they were making a sound and responsible social decision. Not everything people may want can necessarily be provided in a world of limited resources, thus trade-offs have to be made and Ford made a rational economic decision. A decision that within its own contextual ideological framework was appropriate and socially responsible because it was made within the assumptions and value system of the neoclassical economic model in which Ford visualized its existence. After the fact information about bad publicity and loss of good will might show that Ford miscalculated the cost of not redesigning the Pinto fuel system but such a position only asserts that they failed to fully appreciate or account for all of the costs and benefits needed in their calculation. Such a criticism does not go to the basic ideological assumptions under which the Ford decision was made, it only goes to the accuracy of their calculation within their chosen belief system.

A problem with the Ford system of decision making is that it inherently must reduce all factors to be considered to a common denominator. As a consequence, human life and personal injuries must be given a dollar equivalent so that it can be compared with the dollar costs to redesign the Pinto. Classical liberal ideology, with its belief in natural and inalienable rights, recognizes that the value of human life cannot be quantified in the way that dishwashers and automobiles are priced for consumption. Respect for individual liberty and human dignity require a recognition of the need for moral dialogue separate and apart from the analysis of costs and benefits in a purely neoclassical economic sense.

Liberals and left-communitarians would also have difficulty with the Ford approach. Ford could be thought of as a large corporation with tremendous economic power, able to exploit the consuming public by denying it access to good and full information and by manipulating the market to ensure sales and profits for its knowingly defective product. From this perspective consumers lack bargaining power and information. They are without access to meaningful alternative choices and Ford takes advantage of them in an effort to maximize profit. In such a setting there is no equality of bargaining power, no equality of treatment, and thus no effective compliance with the demands of the liberal state. Furthermore, the critics from the left communitarian perspective could easily point to the invocation of neoclassical economic theory as a mere legitimizing mythology to justify the illegitimate hierarchy of Ford (capitalist) dominance in our society.

The Court in this case relies on tort law negligence and strict liability rules to hold Ford liable for the injuries caused to the plaintiffs in *Grimshaw*. In so holding, the court adopts, as an unexpressed element of its determination, a rejection of the normative values and assumptions of Ford's ideological vision. In the choice of legal text and the selection of governing legal principles applied to this case the court rejects one world view for another, accepts one ideology, one economic view of social relationships, over that of another. In this sense every judicial decision involves a philosophical choice. The important point is to be able to assess these underlying values in order to see that "good" and "bad", "just" and "unjust", etc., are terms that are inherently contingent with respect to the ideological context in which the actors operate. Recognizing this simple point will make us better lawyers.

Suggested Reading

Books

W. Prosser & W. Keeton, THE LAW OF TORTS (5th ed. 1984).

R. Rabin, PERSPECTIVES ON TORT LAW (2d. ed. 1983).

L. Strobel, RECKLESS HOMICIDE? (1980).

Articles

Calabresi, *Some Thoughts on Risk Distribution and the Law of Torts,* 70 YALE L.J. 499 (1961).

Fried, *The Value of Life,* 82 HARV.L.REV. 1415 (1969).

Jones–Lee, *The Value of Changes in the Probability of Death or Injury,* 82 J.POL.ECON. 835 (1974).

Kennedy, *Distributive and Paternalist Motives in Contract and Tort Law, with Special References to Compulsory Terms and Unequal Bargaining Power,* 41 MD.L.REV. 563 (1982).

Landes & Posner, *The Positive Economic Theory of Tort Law,* 15 GA.L.REV. 851 (1981).

Malloy, *Equating Human Rights and Property Rights— The Need for Moral Judgment in an Economic Analysis of Law and Social Policy,* 47 OHIO ST.L.J. 163 (1986).

Rhoads, *How Much Should We Spend to Save a Life?* 51 PUB.INTEREST 74 (1978).

Rabin, *The Historical Development of the Fault Principle: A Reinterpretation,* 15 GA.L.REV. 925 (1981).

Steiner, *Economics, Morality, and the Law of Torts,* 26 U.TORONTO L.J. 227 (1976).

Part Four
CONCLUDING MATERIALS

Chapter Fourteen

IMPROVING LAWYERING SKILLS

The goal of this book has been to provide a broad based introduction to the relationship between law and economics. While coverage of any particular approach to the study of law and economics is restricted in a book of this size and type, every effort has been made to provide, through text and extensive suggested reading lists, a framework for basic understanding and a basis for further study.

The primary thesis of the book has been to demonstrate the need for lawyers and all students of the law to be able to deal with economic, political, and ideological issues when thinking about the law and legal institutions. In today's legal environment the competent lawyer must not only be able to recharacterize legal problems between different sets of legal rules, he must also be able to shift legal dialogue between alternative economic approaches. As an example, consider the real property lawyer's skill in recharacterizing a long-term land sale contract into a lease arrangement or into a constructive fee transfer subject to a mortgage. The ability to recharacterize the legal problem from one sounding in contract to one based on a landlord and tenant relationship or one based on mortgage law allows the lawyer to seek out the most favorable legal doctrines, remedies, and protections for her client. For the competent lawyer these skills, while still important, are not enough. Now, every competent lawyer needs to know how to properly frame the philosophical understanding of their client's case. For some judges a contract unconscionability case needs to be framed in terms of evidence about market competition or the lack thereof, whereas for other judges the proper presentation of the case requires a focus on the educational achievement of the aggrieved party, income information, relative bargaining power, and etc. (See Chapters 9 and 10).

With respect to judges this task of learning how to frame a case becomes increasingly a matter of study with the added research assistance of such services as WESTLAW. Such data base systems allow researchers to select a search of a particular judge's prior decisions on specific types of legal, political, or economic issues. Thus, it is possible to learn a great deal about a particular judge's viewpoint in addition to using such services to do more traditional legal research.

In this book emphasis has been put on showing a practical application for the lawyer in structuring or understanding judicial opinions. The focus on judicial opinions is meant to provide easy and tangible illustrations of some of the points raised in the book. In reality, however, the key to understanding the implications of this book is to realize that the judges are just a small subset example of a much broader audience. You may be trying to understand or make an argument to an arbitration panel, a legislative body, a newspaper editor, a city commission, an opposing counsel, a classroom of your peers, or perhaps just a friend. In anyone of these or other potential situations you must always be aware of the idea that "facts", words, text, context, fairness, justice, etc., are concepts that are contingent. They have potentially different subjective meanings to people of different economic, political, and ideological perspectives. It is important, therefore, that as lawyers, we begin to appreciate these differences, that we begin to appreciate the complexity of our social situation, and that we learn to deal with law, not as an autonomous field of scientific study, but as an integral part of an interdisciplinary understanding of the human experience.

If this book has helped to introduce this idea of law and of a comparative approach to law and economics it will have been successful. While the "real world" can seldom be broken down into neat attempts at separating distinct ideological theories of law and of economics the attempt here has been to show the implication of these ideas at work in the struggle over the ascendancy of competing and often times conflicting and unspoken assumption about the nature and meaning of the "good" society and the relationship of the individual, the community, the state, the law, and economics to that "good" society.

Suggested Reading

Books

L. Boff & C. Boff, Introducing Liberation Theology (1987).

A. Chafuen, Christians for Freedom—Late Scholastic Economics (1986).

Economic Liberties and the Judiciary (J. Dorn & H. Manne ed. 1987).

R. Heilbroner, The Nature and Logic of Capitalism (1985).

M. Lutz & K. Lux, Humanistic Economics: the New Challenge (1988).

C. Menger, Principles of Economics (1976).

L. Mises, Human Action: a Treatise on Economics (1963).

National Conference of Catholic Bishops, Economic Justice for All (1986).

M. Novak, Will it Liberate?: Questions About Liberation Theology (1986).

E. Schumacher, Small Is Beautiful: Economics as if People Mattered (1973).

A. Shand, The Capitalist Alternative: an Introduction to Neo–Austrian Economics (1984).

T. Sowell, A Conflict of Visions: Ideological Origins of Political Struggles (1987).

T. Veblen, The Theory of the Leisure Class (1953).

Articles

Constitutional Protections of Economic Activity: How They Promote Individual Freedom, 11 Geo.Mason U.L.Rev. 1 (1988).

Easterbrook, *The Court and the Economic System,* 98 Harv.L.Rev. 4 (1984).

Babcock, *Economists on the Bench,* 50 L. & Contemp. Prob. 1 (1987).

Ellickson, *A Critique of Economic and Sociological Theories of Social Control,* 16 J.Legal Stud. 67 (1987).

Lowi, *Two Roads to Serfdom: Liberalism, Conservatism and Administrative Power,* 36 Am.U.L.R. 295 (1987).

Markovits, *Pursuing One's Rights Under Socialism,* 38 Stan.L.Rev. 689 (1986).

McBride, *The Fetishism of Illegality and the Mystifications of "Authority" and "Legitimacy",* 18 Ga.L. Rev. 863 (1984).

McFarland, *Interest Groups and Theories of Power in America,* 17 B.J.Pol.S. 129 (1987).

Non–Posnerian Law and Economics Symposium, 12 Hamline L.Rev. 1 (1988).

Novak, *The Liberal Society As Liberation Theology,* 2 N.D.J.L., Ethics & Pub.Pol'y. 27 (1985).

Posner, *The Decline of Law as an Autonomous Discipline: 1962–1987,* 100 Harv.L.Rev. 761 (1987).

Rosenfeld, *Contrast and Justice: The Relation Between Classical Contract Law and Social Contract Theory,* 70 Iowa L.R. 769 (1985)

Sensat, *Methodological Individualism and Marxism,* 4 Econ. & Phil. 189 (1988).

Stone, *Theories of Law and Justice of Fascist Italy,* 1 Modern L.R. 177 (1937).

Symposium on Post-Chicago Law and Economics, 65 Chi.–Kent L.Rev. 3 (1989).

GLOSSARY

Arrow's Impossibility Theorem—Society's choices must satisfy four conditions in order to reflect the preferences of the individuals comprising society, but it is impossible to make a choice among all sets of alternatives without violating at least one of these conditions. The four conditions are: (1) social choices must be transitive; (2) social choices must not respond in an opposite direction to changes in individual choice; (3) social choices must not be dictated by anyone inside or outside the society; and (4) the social preference between two alternatives must depend only on people's feelings regarding those two alternatives and not on their opinion of other alternatives.

Coase's Theorem—Theory that a competitive society can still allocate resources efficiently in spite of externalities provided the costs of the negotiations are small.

Complementary Goods—A pair of goods having the property that an increase in the price of one results in a decrease in demand for the other.

Demand Curve—Represents the amount of goods that consumers will be willing to buy at a given price.

Economics—The study of human actions in a social context, especially as those actions are directed toward the use of scarce resources to satisfy potentially unlimited wants.

Efficiency—The property of acting with a minimum of expense, effort, and waste.

Kaldor–Hicks Theory—Concerned only with whether or not society's aggregate utility has been maximized, and therefore believes a reallocation of resources is efficient if those who gain from it obtain enough to fully compensate those who lose from it.

Marginal Cost—The increase in cost required to increase output of some good or service by one unit.

Marginal Utility—The additional utility a person receives from consuming one additional unit of a good.

Opportunity Cost—The cost of doing something measured in terms of the lost value of doing the next best alternative with the same time or resources.

Pareto Optimum—A situation where it is impossible to make any Pareto improvement. That is, it is impossible to make any individual better off without making someone else worse off.

Pareto Superiority—Making one person better off without making anyone else worse off.

Production Possibility Curve—A curve showing the possible combinations of goods that can be produced by an economy, given available resources and technology.

Rationality—Means that in the choice process confronting us because of scarcity, people will act in a manner that they believe gives them the best combination of desirable results within the confines of their resources.

Scarcity—The potentially unlimited nature of human wants as compared with the limited nature of available resources.

Substitute Goods—A pair of goods having the property that an increase in the price of one results in a decrease in the price of the other.

Supply Curve—Represents the amount of goods that will be supplied to a market at a given price.

Transaction Costs—Conditions impeding the carrying out of mutually beneficial exchanges; such costs include information costs, costs of negotiating and contracting, and costs imposed by taxes and regulations.

*

Index

†